The State and Local Government Workers'
RETIREMENT SAVINGS GUIDE

BRUCE S. STUART

Dearborn™
Trade Publishing
A **Kaplan Professional** Company

Vice President and Publisher: Cynthia A. Zigmund
Editorial Director: Donald J. Hull
Senior Project Editor: Trey Thoelcke
Interior Design: Lucy Jenkins
Cover Design: Scott Rattray, Rattray Designs
Typesetting: the dotted i

Published by Dearborn Trade Publishing, a Kaplan Professional Company

Printed in the United States of America

02   03   04   10   9   8   7   6   5   4   3   2   1

Library of Congress Cataloging-in-Publication Data

Stuart, Bruce S., 1964–
    The state and local government workers' retirement savings guide / Bruce S. Stuart.
        p.   cm.
    Includes index.
    ISBN 0-7931-5951-2
    1. State governments—Officials and employees—Pensions—United States.   2. State governments—Officials and employees—Retirement—United States—Planning.   3. Local officials and employees—Pensions—United States.   4. Local officials and employees—Retirement—United States—Planning.   I. Title.
    JK2474 .S78 2002
    332.024'01—dc21
                                                                        2002010499

DEDICATION

This book is dedicated to my parents Vernon and Suellen Stuart who taught me that success in life is not measured by what you know or even whom you know, but rather what you do for others and whom you can help. If this book helps to make your life even a little easier, I have succeeded.

CONTENTS

ACKNOWLEDGMENTS

*D*on Hull, Editorial Director of Dearborn Trade Publishing, an outstanding editor and a heck of a great guy!

Courtney Goethals, publicist; Leslie Banks, Marketing Director; and Robin Bermel, Special Sales Director at Dearborn Trade have each worked diligently to make sure that this book is in the public's eye.

Sheree Bykofsky, a truly warm, kind, caring, and thoroughly knowledgeable literary agent and her associate Megan Buckley, a superefficient, bright, and personable woman with a great sense of humor.

Trey Thoelcke, Project Editor at Dearborn Trade, astutely made certain all production deadlines were met.

Dawn Chamberlain at Albany Law School, a person who really takes an interest in others and who has been a true friend.

Kevin Thomas Kitchin, a dynamic and inspirational mentor.

Bonnie Johnson and Casey Murphy, two great ladies who have always been there with super ideas and kindness.

Maryanne Moxie, Lia Lundgren, August Urgola, Joseph Glucksnis, Thomas Ferrari, Jeff Huester, and Peggy Tikrani, a phenomenally skilled and exceptionally well-versed group of individuals with whom I have had great pleasure working.

Professor Sandra Stevenson, a brilliant, supportive, creative, and patient educator and friend.

Professor Patricia Salkin, the dynamic Director of the Government Law Center at Albany Law School, who took the time to guide me in locating information for this book.

Helen Adams-Keane, Director of Alumni Affairs, Albany Law School, for all of her help.

Sandra Mans at Albany Law School, Assistant Dean for Career Planning, who guided me in the right direction.

Andrea Oberle at Peace Officers Research Association of California (PORAC), an incredibly bright and meticulous woman who steered me in the right direction regarding further research about safety personnel.

Barbara Wolf, John Marshall Burke, and John Ritchie, who provided sound advice, creative input, and friendship throughout the creative process of this book.

Paul E. Kuntne, who gave direction in researching fixed income.

Howard Adler, Nancy Adler, Cynthia Allison, Clem Amorose, Karen Butler, Lisa Barry, Sheila Barry, Clay Bedford, Bonnie Bennetts, Thomas Bevilacqua, Kathleen Boland, Judy Cannon, Isabel Carrasco, Robert Chapman, John Concepion, Marsha

Cook, Virginia Cooke, Fran Cowey, Raymond Cox, Ann Del Rosario, Karen Dewees, Marife Elmore, Ester Feder, Alex Fielding, Sarah Fielding, Rod Foster, Phyllis Gibson, Craig Green, Daniel and Olivia Haley, Helen Harris, R. Malcolm Hendry, David Hodgkins, Eleanor Hollywood, LaCarre Ivy, Betty Jacobs, Beth Johnson, Jeff Johnson, Suzanne Lavin, Marca Lamore, Bobbie Larkins, Harold Majorca, Robert Maron, Maria Martinez, Jorge Martinez, Jordan Matthews, Julio Mendoza, Millicent Miles, Rosemary Miller, Regina Moreno, Jonathon Muhiudeen, Judith Nevitt, Elyse Papp, Melissa Parker, Barbara Perry, Regina Ravetti, Beth Remick, Leo Reyes, Lawrence Sasaki, Douglas Schearer, Paul Schieber, Kathleen Schneibel, Steve Scott, Marcela and Randy Serafini, Nicki Spillane, Dan Spradling, Joannie Stewart-Miller, Kim Stuart-Fielding, John Tagliaferi, Harvey Tureck, Frank Vargas, Marge Ann Vrooman, Fred Woerner, and Dolores Wright, friends who have exhibited the very best traits we cherish in the human race.

And last but far from least, my clients who on many occasions have asked me why I work so hard staying in the office past 6 PM and on weekends and working from 6 AM to 10 PM for police (to cover all shifts) and on weekends for firefighters. I can confess now, I have worked so hard for you because each of you has always made me feel special and I wanted you to feel special as well.

CHAPTER 1

SHHH . . . DON'T TELL YOUR PRIVATE SECTOR FRIENDS

*T*here are quite a few books written about retirement for your friends and colleagues in the private sector, but until now there have been no books written about retirement planning specifically for you—the state, local, or county government worker. So, when I set out to write this book, I decided I wanted to make it very special. I wanted to create a book that brings financial concepts and terms to life in a slightly different way than had ever been done before.

In fact, many of the areas addressed in this book haven't been discussed in other retirement books or, at most, only have been touched upon lightly. So, as you sit back and take a journey with me through this world of the government worker's retirement investing and planning, think about your private sector friends. If they knew about this book they might be a little bit jealous. But remember, this book has been designed just for you, the government worker.

SO, LET'S TALK ABOUT YOU

Why do you perform the work you do? Is it for the money or the sense of satisfaction you derive from carrying out your duties and hopefully helping others? Decades ago, in his ground-breaking book, *Working*, Studs Terkel interwove the threads of both job challenges and satisfaction teased out from myriad workers in the private and public sectors. (*Working* by Studs Terkel. New York: The Free Press, 1974.)

Inevitably, whenever I talk with state, county, and local government employees, the top reasons why they selected their jobs included the enjoyment from their work, the security of their position, and the retirement benefits. So, with retirement benefits of such great importance to this group, you would assume that there would be several books designed to help them with their retirement benefits. I assumed that these books existed too. That was until many of these employees asked me where they could buy one of these books. The surprising result was that I couldn't find any books specifically targeted toward the retirement planning needs of state, county, and local employees.

The State and Local Government Worker's Retirement Savings Guide is designed to help you better plan your retirement while taking into consideration the specific needs of the government employee. Everything presented in this book is designed to make your life a little bit easier by carefully explaining hard-to-understand and, dare we say, tedious material in a fun and more accessible manner.

Let's begin with a road map detailing how this book is organized so you can find the information you need more rapidly. The following road posts will guide you along with the basic narrative text, as you use this book.

HOW DOES IT WORK? *These sections will explain the nuts and bolts of each major concept that you need to understand in order to coordinate your government retirement. You will find that these sections will make difficult-to-understand concepts easier and even fun. Before you can truly master the ins and outs of putting your government retirement strategy together, you must understand these basic terms.*

A CAPITAL IDEA. *Think of these sections as the finer shading that an artist adds once she has sketched a preliminary drawing of a subject. These finer details will strengthen your government retirement strategy by providing you with proven ways to get the most out of your careful retirement planning.*

PUBLIC WORKING KNOWLEDGE. *These sections provide interesting facts relating to the topics in which they are found. They may be derived from history or a recent factoid from a United States municipality. For example, in discussions designed for safety personnel, you will learn not only that progressive city Sunnyvale, California, cross-trains both fire and police to perform each other's jobs, but also that cardiac arrest is a leading cause of firefighter disability in the United States.*

UNCLE SAM'S CUT. *These sections will let you know how much you will pay in taxes on a given retirement savings plan in the event that you either withdraw early (if you are able to do so) or are officially able to take it out based on the IRS's rules.*

THE BOTTOM LINE. *Sometimes when you are reading a book, you just want the "take home" message that the author is trying to get across so you can go back later and fill in the details. This section will highlight these no-nonsense encapsulations. I would caution you that to fully understand what you are doing with your government retirement, you should not simply read these sections as a substitute for reading the entire book. As you will quickly realize by delving into this material, there is a lot that you need to know and just reading a few summaries is not going to get you where you want to be in the long run.*

LIFE OR POLICY? *In Chapter 2 of this book, you will be introduced to insurance and its uses both in the government workplace and after you retire. These sections will provide further information about insurance for the remainder of this book.*

FOR YOUR REFERENCE. *There is a tremendous amount of information that you need to understand regarding your government retirement savings. In these sections, additional resources including books, periodicals, and Web sites are included so you may explore any of these subjects in greater detail at your own pace.*

SOUNDS LIKE A PLAN. *In the Sounds like a Plan sections, you will learn the strategies you may wish to design for your government retirement by following the problems and solutions for several different fic-*

tional state and local government employees. *These scenarios highlight much of the information you have read about in the sections in which they appear, and apply this information to real-life situations.*

Me Pages

In creating this book, I wanted you to use it as a reference, but I also wanted you to interact with it and make it your very own book. For that reason, each section of this book has Me Pages, which are designed to gather information about your current government retirement situation. The final chapter of this book includes additional Me Pages on which you can compile all your information for review on your own or with a financial advisor as you structure your individual government retirement strategy.

THE BEST WAY TO USE THIS BOOK

When you start reading this book, the temptation may be to skim over much of the material presented and focus solely on the sections that contain information you currently need. Additionally, you may be tempted to avoid sections for safety personnel and/or the highly compensated employee if you feel that you do not fit into these categories. Read them anyway. Many of the ideas contained in these chapters will help you even if you do not consider yourself part of these groups.

For example, you do not have to be a firefighter or a police officer to set up investment teams or form an alliance with an investment buddy, concepts explained in Chapter 8. You also do not have to be a highly compensated government employee to learn how to select a full-service financial advisor, which is explained in Chapter 7.

Some Great Web Sites for State and Local Government Employees

As you will soon learn while you read this book, there are a number of Web sites and other references provided for you. But before you even look at those, here are a few basic government Web sites that you should examine:

- *Google.com/UncleSam* <www.google.com/unclesam> Little did you know that one of the Internet's best search engines can also be tailor-made into a government information retrieval site simply by adding *unclesam* at the end of the Web address.

- *GovSpot* <www.govspot.com> This is an outstanding Web site devoted to all sections of government employment including state and local government. The site contains information about jobs as well as trivia and a number of other topics of interest to state and local government employees.

- *FirstGov* <www.firstgov.gov/government/services.shtml> FirstGov provides a variety of links including the Government Gateway, which is of special use to state and local government employees.

- *Government Technology* <www.govtech.net> Government Technology is specifically designed for state and government employees seeking technology solutions.

- *International City/County Management Association (ICMA)* <www.icma.org> This organization represents appointed managers and administrators of local governments internationally.

- *National Association of Counties* <www.naco.org> The National Association of Counties was created in 1935 and has a membership of over 2,000 counties in the United States. This organization provides legislative, research, and a number of services to its members and serves as a national advocate for counties.

- *National Association of Government Defined Contribution Administrators (NAGDCA)* <www.nagdca.org> NAGDCA has two primary missions. First, to serve as an educational forum for state and local governments and private sector organizations providing defined contribution plans. Second, NAGDCA serves as an advocate for federal legislation that will advance retirement plans.

- *National League of Cities* <www.nlc.org> The National League of Cities provides research, educational conferences, and a number of other services to its members that consist of approximately 1,800 cities, towns, and villages of varying sizes.

CHAPTER 2

PENDULUMS, PYRAMIDS, AND THE UNEXPECTED

The Basics of Investing and Insurance

*B*efore any discussion of retirement strategies, we must make sure that we are all on the same page. There are certain basic investment and insurance concepts which you must understand so that it is easier for you to either manage your government retirement planning yourself or work with a financial professional.

THE PENDULUMS

In the corner of my parent's living room, there sits an enormous mahogany grandfather clock with a timeworn face segmented into 12 equal parts. When I was a boy, I used to sit on the couch across from the clock and watch its pendulum swing back and forth marking time. The investments you have in your government retirement plan are very much like that pendulum swinging back and forth depending on the strength of the market. The more aggressive investments will swing far wider in both the upward and downward directions. Other investments, such as the guaranteed interest account, which we will discuss later, will almost appear to be frozen in time. What we will ultimately want to do is create the proper clockwork movement for your entire government retirement portfolio balancing these pendulums depending on your individual circumstances. Let's talk about these pendulums one by one.

Stocks: The Speed Boats

The one thing that has surprised me most is that despite the tremendous media attention paid to stocks and the stock market, many investors do not understand the basic underpinnings of these investments in which they are placing their hard-earned monies from each paycheck.

A stock is part ownership in a publicly traded company. Whenever you buy a share of stock in a company such as General Motors, IBM, or Washington Post (the parent corporation of the publisher of this book), you are buying something which can stay the same in value, plummet to zero, or increase to infinity.

 HOW DOES IT WORK? *Stocks are often hard for people to understand because they are intangibles. You can't actually reach out and*

physically touch IBM or Merck Pharmaceuticals. So, let's equate stocks to something you can actually visualize. Think of a stock as a speed boat. The water underneath it is the market. Picture the speed boat in your mind. What happens to it if the water is really smooth and you have a well-built boat with a high-powered engine? You will move across the water rather rapidly. Right?

Now imagine that the water underneath is very choppy. Your speed boat is going to go up and down and bounce all over the place. Isn't it? The same is true with stocks. They are very dependent on the overall stock market, particularly the sector in which they are located. Examples of sectors are financials, technology, and health care. If a particular sector is performing poorly, the value of stocks within that sector may be adversely impacted. Based on the analogy of the speed boat, realize that the value of stocks can move quickly either upward or downward.

A CAPITAL IDEA. There are both common stocks and preferred stocks. Most of us have greater experience with common stocks which grant voting rights in a company and are bought primarily for appreciation in value and/or for periodic payments derived from the company's earnings, known as dividends. Preferred stocks generally don't give you any voting rights, but in the event that the company goes bankrupt, the preferred shareholder (the person who owns the stock) gets paid before the common stock shareholder. Preferred stocks combine the elements of stocks and bonds in that they trade on the market like stocks but have features similar to bonds like being rated for credit quality and paying a periodic yield such as 7 percent per year. Preferreds can also fluctuate in value like common stocks, but their share prices are generally not as volatile.

Company Stock

Due to the horrific aftermath Enron workers experienced because they had large percentages of company stock in their 401(k)s, there has been a call for massive reforms regarding company stock in retirement savings plans. Company stock is stock from the corporation for which the employee works. As a public sector employee, you will not have any company stock because the government does not issue stock.

THE BOTTOM LINE. *Stocks are part ownership in a corporation. If the market is doing well and you are in the right stock, you will do very well. However, if the market is performing poorly you may take a greater hit.*

PUBLIC WORKING KNOWLEDGE. *In Berkeley, California, many city employees have sung with me about financial terms including a song which I created called "P.E." Following are the lyrics to "P.E." We will go into a greater discussion of growth and value a little later when we discuss mutual funds.*

P.E. (Price to Earnings Ratio)
When you're picking stocks
Trying to avoid shocks
There's something you should be learnin'
It's stock price over earnings
P.E. . . . It's not just gym class anymore
P.E. . . . It's what you should be looking for
Divide the current stock price

By how much the company made

The number you come up with

Tells a lot about the price you just paid

Low price and high earnings

That's what Value buyers are yearnin'

Growth buyers don't worry about today's P.E.

They're bankin' on where the company'll be

P.E. . . . . It's not just gym class anymore

P.E. . . . . It's what you should be lookin' for

P.E. ©1999 Bruce Stuart

Other Criteria Used to Evaluate Stocks

Several ratios are used by analysts and investors to determine stock value. One of the ones is the price-earnings (PE) ratio. You can get this ratio by dividing the market price of a share of stock by its earnings per share. If you wish to further explore the value of a particular company, you can also calculate the stock's price-to-earnings/growth (PEG) ratio. To determine a company's PEG ratio, simply divide its PE ratio by its expected rate of growth. This ratio allows you to compare companies that have different growth rates.

You may also wish to explore the profitability of a company. Net profit margin is a company's earnings after taxes divided by its sales. Return on equity (ROE) is a key ratio used in examining a company's profitability, which is measured by a company's earnings after tax divided by its equity.

FOR YOUR REFERENCE. *There are a number of outstanding books and Web sites about stocks and stock selection. Here are a few with which you should be familiar.*

Books:

- How to Buy Stocks *by Louis Engel and Henry B. Hecht. Boston: Little, Brown & Co., 1994.*

- One Up on Wall Street *by Peter Lynch with John Rothchild. New York: Fireside/Simon & Schuster, 1989.*

- The Psychology of Investing *by Lawrence E. Lifson and Richard A. Geist. New York: John Wiley & Sons, 1999.*

- SmartMoney Stock Picker's Bible *by Huang Finch. New York: John Wiley & Sons, 2002.*

- Using Technical Analysis: A Step-By-Step Guide to Understanding and Applying Stock Market Charting Techniques *by Clifford Pistolese. New York: McGraw Hill, 1994.*

- The Warren Buffet Way *by Robert G. Hagstrom, Jr. New York: John Wiley & Sons, 1995.*

- Value Investing *(4th Revised Edition) by Benjamin Graham. New York: HarperBusiness, 1997.*

Web Sites:

- *<www.dorseywright.com> An outstanding source for individual stock research.*

- *<www.thestreet.com> Up-to-date commentary regarding market trends and individual stocks.*

Bonds: The IOUs

Even more so than with stocks, many investors are intimidated or baffled by bonds. There is nothing mystical about bonds. They are simply a way of creating a fixed income, something that will pay you a set rate of return for a certain time period.

HOW DO THEY WORK? *Once again, we want to turn the intangible idea into something you can touch. Take out a sheet of paper and write the letters IOU on it. This piece of paper is a bond. When an entity such as a local government (municipal bonds), corporation (corporate bonds), or the United States government (treasuries) needs money, they sell bonds stating that they will be paying the debt off in a number of years and that in return for the loan they will give the bond holder a certain amount of interest periodically.*

When investing using individual bonds, it is important to understand certain bond terms. Coupon, yield, yield to maturity, and call date(s) are all key features of bonds. The coupon for a bond is the percent amount which the bond promises to pay you at a set date, often annually or semiannually. If a bond has a 10 percent coupon and is worth $1,000 at its face value, that means you should be getting $100 each year, or two payments of $50 every six months. The yield to maturity for the bond is the percentage return you will get from the bond if you hold it until it is due. For example, if it is 2002 and you hold a five-year bond, it will be due in 2007. The amount of return you will receive from this bond between 2002 and 2007 is known as the yield to maturity. This amount takes into consideration the fact that you may have either paid a premium for your bond or your bond may have traded at a discount when you bought it.

Now, what if the issuer of the bond has the right to prepay or call the bond in 2005? That means your bond may be called in three years, and at that time you will receive the prestated call value of your bond. Your percentage return on the bond between the time you first buy it and when the bond is called by its issuer, taking into consideration how much you paid and how much you will receive if the bond is called, is known as the yield to call.

Another measure of what you may yield from your bond is the yield to worst. This yield factors in all possible scenarios, such as the various yields to call you may receive if there are multiple dates when the bond can be called. It then compares the various yields with the yield to maturity to figure out the worst possible yield for the bond. The cautious investor in individual bonds is well advised to examine the yield to worst for his or her bond, along with factors including the bond's coupon, credit rating(s), yield to call, and yield to maturity.

A CAPITAL IDEA. *Let's assume that your Great Aunt Fanny recently passed away and left you a $10,000 municipal bond yielding 5 percent that is due in ten years. What does this mean to you? It means that that municipality is giving you its word or* its bond *that it will repay you the $10,000 you loaned to it at the end of ten years with 5 percent interest or a total of $500 paid to you each year until the bond matures or is due. Is this all you should know about the bond? Nope.*

Whenever you have a bond, you should look very carefully at the credit quality of the bond issuer. Think of it as if you've been hit up for a loan by someone you know. If your friend has declared bankruptcy three times in the last year and comes to you for a loan, do you want to give it to him? I don't think so! The same is true with a bond issuer. The better the credit quality, the more likely your bond issuer will pay you your monies due on time and will not default. If they default on the bond, you may lose some or all of your investment.

Most people can understand the idea that a bond is an IOU. What they generally have a hard time with is that bonds can fluctuate in value just as stocks do. Let's assume you have that $10,000 municipal bond from Great Aunt Fanny. You need that bond money to buy a car! Since your Great Aunt Fanny bought the bond, interest rates have gone up and now more attractive bonds are out there for the bond buyer. Thus, your bond, which you need to sell before it is due, has gone down in value.

Conversely, if your bond becomes more attractive because it is paying a higher rate than current bonds being issued or the credit quality has gone up, you will have a more valuable bond if you chose to sell it before it is due. If you hold it until its due date you will get the face value of the bond plus any accrued interest. In this example, if you sell the bond anytime after ten years, you will receive your original $10,000 plus the $5,000 interest that accrued during those ten years.

Types of Bonds

There are many different types of bonds including corporate bonds which are issued by a corporation, municipal bonds which are issued by a municipality, U.S. government bonds such as Treasury bonds, agency bonds which are backed by the full faith credit of a government agency, and mortgage backed bonds.

HOW DOES IT WORK? Corporate Bonds. *Corporate bonds are IOUs issued by a corporation, such as Ford Motor Company or Bank of America, when it is trying to raise working capital. Even if you do not invest in individual bonds you may find corporate bonds in your bond or bal-*

anced mutual funds. If you are buying individual corporate bonds you should look carefully at all of the features discussed above.

 UNCLE SAM'S CUT. Keep in mind that in your nonretirement accounts that the yield from corporate bonds, as well as any capital appreciation (if the bond goes up in value and you sell it), is taxable.

 HOW DOES IT WORK? Treasuries. You may have seen a government income mutual fund in your deferred compensation portfolio and wondered what was in it. Often these funds are invested in treasuries that come in different durations. U.S. Treasury Bonds are IOUs of ten year or greater duration that are backed by the full faith and credit of the U.S. government. Treasury Notes are also IOUs of the U.S. government, which have a maturity less than ten years.

 UNCLE SAM'S CUT. Treasury bonds and notes are federally taxable and state exempt in nonretirement accounts.

 HOW DOES IT WORK? High-Yield Bonds. These are the IOUs from entities that are not as creditworthy and thus have poorer credit quality. As a result of this poorer credit quality, these bonds have a higher chance of defaulting and are a higher risk investment. Unless you are experienced with this form of investment, you are generally better served turning it over to a professional, such as a high-yield bond fund.

 HOW DOES IT WORK? Municipal Bonds. A municipal bond is just what it sounds like. It is an IOU issued by a municipality be it for a roadway or a utility plant that they need money to build. The advantage these bonds have is that they are double (or triple depending on where you *live) tax exempt for the interest which you are paid provided that you live in the same state from which the bond is issued. Also realize that Puerto Rico is a "wild card." You can use Puerto Rico (or any other U.S. territory) bonds as a substitute for your own state's muni bonds and still get the tax break.*

UNCLE SAM'S CUT. *Please realize that although the money you get in interest payments from municipal bonds is tax exempt, if the bond itself goes up in value and you sell it for a capital gain before it is due, that capital appreciation of the bond is still taxable.*

A CAPITAL IDEA. Should you use municipal bonds in your retirement portfolio? Generally, municipal bonds pay lower rates of return than non-tax-advantaged bonds. As a group, they carry far less risk than their corporate bond counterparts, but because you will be investing in plans which are already tax advantaged these bonds will not help you as much. If you are in a high tax bracket, it is better to use municipal bonds in your taxable investment accounts.

FOR YOUR REFERENCE. The following are some excellent books about bonds:

- Bond Market Rules: 50 Investing Axioms to Master Bonds for Income or Trading *by Michael D. Sheimo. New York: McGraw Hill, 2000.*

- The Bond Bible *by Marilyn Cohen with Nick Watson. Paramus: New York Institute of Finance, 2000.*

- Getting Started in Bonds *by Michael C. Thomsett. New York: John Wiley & Sons, 1991.*

- The Handbook of Mortgage Backed Securities *(5th Edition) by Frank J. Fabozzi (Editor). New York: McGraw Hill, 2001*

- Inside the Yield Book *by Sidney Homer and Martin L. Leibowitz, PhD. Paramus: New York Institute of Finance, 1972.*

 THE BOTTOM LINE. *Bonds are nothing more than IOUs issued by entities such as corporations, municipalities, or the U.S. government. They fluctuate in value based on a number of factors including interest rates and the credit quality of the bond issuer.*

Mutual Funds: The Ocean Liners

It is highly likely that when you sit down to assess your government retirement plan statements, you will notice that some of your investments are held in mutual funds. Often these funds will have a company name coupled with other words describing in what kinds of things they are supposed to be investing your money.

 HOW DOES IT WORK? *Mutual funds were first created in 1924 in Massachusetts by a fund company known as MFS. They started a fund named the MFS Massachusetts Investors Trust (a.k.a. the MIT—a fund which still exists today!). A mutual fund is simply a collection of all stocks (an equity fund), all bonds (a bond fund), or part stocks and part bonds (a balanced fund). Mutual funds are designed to create greater diversification for your portfolio than you would obtain by buying an individual stock or bond because there are a greater number of investments housed inside each fund.*

 A CAPITAL IDEA. *Let's return to our physical analogies one more time. The mutual fund is an ocean liner and the water underneath it*

is the market. Will an ocean liner move as rapidly as a speed boat? Generally not. It will plod along and move toward its destination at a somewhat slower pace.

Hopefully, this boat will also not have as great a risk of sinking, although you should realize that even mutual funds can stay the same in value, reduce to zero, or increase to infinite value. They are nothing more than the sum of their working parts be they stocks, bonds, or a combination of both.

Actively Managed Funds

There are many dividing lines for mutual funds. The first division is whether the fund is actively or passively managed. But what does that mean? Basically, an actively managed fund has a person or a group at the helm of the ocean liner setting out the course which the vessel will take. This entity is either called a fund manager or an investment management team.

PUBLIC WORKING KNOWLEDGE. *Because Morningstar reports are the standard in the industry for evaluating mutual funds, it is important that you are aware of recent changes made to these rating systems as of July 2002. The star rating has been changed to be a category-by-category comparison of mutual funds and this evaluative tool is updated on a monthly basis. This change in ratings alleviated the need for the old rating system where 1 was the lowest and 5 was the highest.*

A CAPITAL IDEA. Socially Responsible Investing. *If you like the idea of investing your money in companies that do business in a cer-*

tain manner, you may explore the option of socially responsible investing within your retirement plan. There are a wide variety of both actively and passively managed mutual funds that invest in companies that do not produce alcohol, tobacco, firearms, or conduct animal testing as well as meet many other socially responsible criteria. Some socially responsible funds loaded up on technology stocks during the late 1990s as a means to achieve clean businesses with high profits. As was the case with all tech-heavy funds, this strategy paid off nicely until the bubble burst. It is advisable to closely examine the holdings of your socially responsible fund offerings just as closely as all other funds in your portfolio.

UNCLE SAM'S CUT. *Both actively and passively managed mutual funds may give capital gains distributions at the end of the year. In nonretirement accounts, you may actually have a fund that lost money for which you still owe capital gains taxes. This is known as* phantom gains. *In retirement accounts, you have no capital gains or capital losses while the money is housed inside its tax-deferred structure.*

THE BOTTOM LINE. *Mutual fund investing can be accomplished in a variety of ways. The advantage of mutual funds is that they are generally more diversified than individual stocks or bonds so if the markets have problems, you won't take as much of a hit. All mutual funds (both load and no load) have operational expenses, which are deducted from your returns.*

FOR YOUR REFERENCE. *Mutual fund investing is a national pastime. As a result, there are a large number of resources for mutual fund information. The following is a handpicked grouping of some of the best places to read about mutual funds.*

Newspapers:

- The Wall Street Journal
- Investor's Business Daily

Books:

- Common Sense on Mutual Funds *by John C. Bogle. New York: John Wiley & Sons, 1999.*
- Bogle on Mutual Funds *by John C. Bogle. New York: Dell, 1994.*
- Socially Responsible Investing: Making a Difference and Making Money *by Amy L. Domini. Chicago: Dearborn Financial Publishing, Inc., 2001.*
- But Which Mutual Funds? How to Pick the Right Ones to Achieve Your Financial Dreams *by Steven T. Goldberg. Washington, D.C.: Kiplinger's Books, 1998.*
- Exchange Traded Funds *by Jim Wiandt and Will McClatchy. New York: John Wiley & Sons, 2002.*

Magazines:

- *Kiplinger's* magazine
- *Mutual Fund Magazine*
- *Money* magazine
- *SmartMoney*

Web sites:

- Fund Alarm *<www.fundalarm.com>*
- ICI Mutual Fund Connection *<www.ici.org>*
- Morningstar.com *<www.morningstar.com>*

Three ways of tracking what is happening with your mutual fund's manager are to call the fund itself, ask your plan's rep what is happening with the manager supervising your plan's funds, or check Morningstar.com on the Internet. This is an outstanding and objective Web site which will give you the fund manager's start date managing and highlight when a manager is leaving or a new one is starting.

Types of Investment Styles

Have you ever turned on CNBC and heard one of the anchors questioning a mutual fund manager about growth or value? Did you wonder what these terms mean as you reviewed your statement? Let's review the differences between growth and value investing and see how they fit into your government retirement portfolio.

Growth Funds: "I Want 'Em! I Want 'Em! I'm Gonna Buy 'Em!"

There are several investment styles, but very simply put the two major styles of investing are growth and value. Instead of using a stock fund, let's focus on a pair of pants that you spotted on your last shopping trip to the department store. They were pants you had to have. In fact, they made you look three sizes smaller without cutting off the circulation to your waist! But as you pulled out the neatly placed price tag you found out that they were $150. What do you do? After all, your high school reunion is right around the corner and you'd make one heck of an entrance strutting in with those pants.

Well, you can do two things: You can wait for them to go on sale—if there are any left in your size and at that price by then—or you can pull out that checkbook and say to the commissioned salesperson waiting on you, "I'm gonna make your day. I want 'em! I want 'em! I'm gonna buy 'em!

Value Funds: "I'm Waiting for the Sale!"

Now, let's assume that you decided you could keep in check your vanity and the need to steal the show at your high school reunion. You held up the pants after you tried them on. Sure they made you look great, but the material was so flimsy it probably wouldn't withstand two washings. You do want the pants, but you figure after the hype wears off you can snag a pair on sale for $75. In essence, you have identified what you wanted to buy at a certain price point, in this case $150, and then you waited for it to go on sale for its fair value which you have determined is $75. You're scratching your head now and saying, "Value is so much more logical than growth. Why doesn't everyone invest that way? Why don't people wait for the prices of stocks to go down to a fair value?"

Well, let me tell you a little story about a company named EToys. Truly a brilliant idea followed through with great management. As the Internet started taking off, it looked like we would be boarding up all the traditional retail stores and buying everything on the Web. EToys had no earnings, but no one seemed to care. Its price also had no real correlation to the company's fair market value—only a hope for the future value of the company. But no one seemed to care. This was also the case for

Internet incubator CMGI, which ultimately lost over 89 percent of its value. Everyone wanted to invest or buy these Internet stocks because they assumed if they didn't buy now they'd have to pay more later. These examples epitomize growth stocks.

Then again, had you invested in Yahoo! when it was $6 a share and sold when it went to $300 you would have made quite a tidy profit! It is interesting to note that when growth was the favored style, the vast majority of value funds in the United States were laggards. Of course, then value became fashionable again and growth fell into the backseat. Growth and value are the yin and yang of your portfolio. One really never knows which style will dominate, so it is best to include both.

GARP Funds: Growth at a Reasonable Price

These are also called blend funds. GARP funds focus on buying the current "hot dot" (meaning the hot investment vehicle for a specific time period) by carefully waiting for these stocks to get kicked on their fannies and taking advantage of the lower stock prices.

The trick is correctly forecasting whether these stocks will get back up and regain their value or whether this is the beginning of the end.

? **HOW DOES IT WORK? *Large Cap, Mid Cap, Small Cap: Which Fund Wears Which Cap?*** *Another term often included in mutual fund names is* cap, *which is an abbreviation for capitalization. The capitalization of a publicly traded company is calculated by multiplying the number of outstanding shares of the stock by the most current stock price. For* *example, if a stock is trading for $30 a share and there are 500 million shares outstanding, the company has a $1.5 billion capitalization.*

Funds use different investment categories based on their philosophies. I am often asked about the cut-off points or ranges of capitalization for a small, mid, or large cap funds. This is a difficult question to answer because the cut-off points or ranges will often be entirely different for each fund.

Passively Managed Funds

You may have heard a coworker talking about how he wants to put all of his money into an index fund. But you may not really have understood what that person was talking about. An index fund basically follows the composition of a specific group of stocks such as Standard & Poor's 500 Index fund (S&P 500) which consists of the 500 largest publicly traded companies in America. The composition of these funds will change as companies are taken out of or added to the grouping based on their size. However, there is no one at the helm of the boat making decisions based on market conditions to redirect the boat.

There are several stock indexes which you will hear about a great deal in the media and among your friends. Here are descriptions of the major indexes.

- *The Dow Jones Industrial Average (a.k.a. "The Dow").* A group of 30 blue chip stocks which are selected by the editors of the *Wall Street Journal*. This group includes many of the cornerstone companies in America such as General Electric, McDonald's, and Microsoft.

- *The Nasdaq.* A popular index often discussed when commentators are indicating whether the "market" is up or down. This index consists of a large number of stocks many of which are technology oriented. Unlike the Dow which has the physical presence of the New York Stock Exchange, the Nasdaq really only exists in cyberspace.

- *The S&P 500.* Standard and Poor's 500 Index comprised of the 500 largest publicly traded corporations in America. Many investors assume that this a "safe" way to invest. You should realize that this index has often been more growth oriented and that the stocks from several of these companies may be volatile, especially those in technology.

- *The Russell 2000 Index.* This index is used to measure the performance of small-cap companies.

- *The EAFE Index.* This very well-known index measures European, Australian, and Far East stock markets. It is a good yardstick for measuring international markets.

HOW DOES IT WORK? Mutual Fund Charges. *There are two major expenses that accompany a mutual fund. The first is a commission, found in load funds, which is generally a percentage of the overall amount invested. This load can be paid up front or it can be deferred in the form of a penalty if you move the money out before a set time, usually six or seven years. This penalty usually decreases each year—for example, 6 percent the first year, 5 percent the second year, and so on—until it reaches 0 percent.*

No-load funds do not charge you commissions either up front or deferred. However, both types of funds have operational expenses.

? *HOW DOES IT WORK? **Operational Expenses.** The operational expenses for a mutual fund cover the cost of the stock trades, mutual fund manager salaries, and everything that goes into running the fund including stock and/or bond trades. Operational expenses can vary widely depending on the fund family and the category of the fund. Don't compare all funds' operating expenses as an absolute. Just as you shouldn't compare a graduate student to a kindergartner, you should compare funds only with others in their own category. For example, operational expenses for international stock funds may be higher because of the use of foreign trading desks, whereas bond funds historically have lower operational expenses.*

We will discuss operational expenses in greater depth when we discuss specific retirement plans. For now, just be aware that there are additional expenses charged by your mutual fund company for management costs and expenses for both load and no-load funds. Also note that when you see your fund's percentage return listed for a given period, the fund's operational expenses have already been taken out.

Some (generally loaded) funds also have 12b-1 fees, which are designed to cover the cost of advertising and marketing the funds to consumers. 12b-1 fees are legally not permitted to exceed 1 percent of the fund's assets.

? *HOW DOES IT WORK? **Net Asset Values.** At the end of each trading day (also known as a "trading session"), the value of your mutual fund(s) are recalculated to determine the new Net Asset Value or NAV for the fund(s). Unlike individual stocks, mutual funds are not really designed for faster trading, but rather for longer term investing.*

Exchange Traded Funds (ETFs)

Exchange traded funds debuted a couple of years ago. In fact, you may have heard of a famous ETF—The QQQ—which is an index of Nasdaq stocks.

However, the ability to use these vehicles as investments in your government retirement plan (if it contains a self-directed brokerage account which we will discuss later on) is very new.

HOW DO THEY WORK? *An ETF is just like a mutual fund in that each fund is a collection of stocks. ETFs also have a symbol just like their mutual fund counterparts. However, these funds are more similar to individual stocks in that they actually trade and their overall value continuously recalibrates during the session. Often, these collections of stocks have lower operating expenses than comparable index funds. However, you do pay transactional costs when you buy and sell them.*

HOW DOES IT WORK ? Sharpe Ratios. *The name of the game in investing is to get a high return with low risk. This is what the Sharpe Ratio measures for mutual funds. It is the percentage of a fund's return divided by the amount of risk the fund took to get that return. There are actual mathematically derived Sharpe Ratios for each mutual fund in America which you can generally get from the funds themselves. If you want to get Sharpe Ratios, Morningstar.com also has this data available on its Web site, along with the fund return.*

Stable Value Investments

In your government retirement plan you will often have stable value investments which will actually be referred to by this name or others. Let's take a look at the most common stable value investments. In general, these stable value accounts are often referred to as guaranteed investment contracts (GICs). In your personal retirement account, they are often known as guaranteed interest accounts (GIAs).

HOW DOES IT WORK? Guaranteed Interest Account. *Your government retirement plan may include an investing option known as a guaranteed interest account or GIA. Notice the word* guaranteed *in this investment option. This is more of an insurance product than an investment vehicle because it is guaranteed never to lose value and also to get a certain rate of return.*

This vehicle generally goes up slowly over time. Whenever the stock and bond markets look rocky, plan participants start to head for it faster than you can say, "Oh fudge!" The rate you are paid on your money is set by the company providing this "subaccount" to your plan provider. GIA rates will often be affected by increases and decreases in short-term interest rates, although many GIA products allow you to "lock in" the rate at which you entered the account. You are taking on no risk by being in a GIA, but over time, assuming historical market averages, your returns will be lower than your performance in higher risk investments.

A CAPITAL IDEA. *Let's assume you move $15,000 in a GIA when the GIA is paying 5 percent. Often, you will be locked into that rate for a year or more, even if interest rates go up or down. Check with your individual plan provider or representative to see exactly how your plan provider treats this option.*

 HOW DOES IT WORK? Money Market. *A money market is comprised of shares of a fund each priced at $1 per share without a trans-*

action cost for buying or selling. The rate of return that you are paid fluctuates constantly. It is not a guaranteed account like a GIA. Before you start moving chunks of your money into a money market from a GIA (if your plan allows that), you should compare rates very carefully. If interest rates are low, money market rates can often be far lower than GIA rates.

HOW DOES IT WORK? Certificate of Deposit (CD). *A CD is usually an FDIC-insured way of saving money for retirement. Money is put into the CD for a specific time period and after that time you are paid your interest and you are free either to roll over that money into another CD or to put it in another investment option. Depending on the duration of the CD, the rates offered are tied to current interest rates. Shorter duration CDs are more closely tied to short-term interest rates. You may be penalized for withdrawing your money prematurely from a CD.*

THE PYRAMIDS:
RISK TOLERANCE AND ASSET ALLOCATION

Congratulations. You've made it through the discussion about pendulums. Now it's time to work on climbing the pyramids. Whenever you hear people refer to *asset allocation*, they are referring to ways to arrange the pendulums we just discussed. The most important thing is to make certain that your portfolio is all about you. You want to take all of your specific biographical information into consideration as you plan your government retirement strategy. So, get out a pen and fill out the basic biographical information on My First Me Page.

My First Me Page

It's All about Me

1. My name is _____.

2. I am _____ years old.

3. Today's date is _____.

4. The municipality where I currently work is _____.

5. My current job title is _____.

6. I am ( ) appointed ( ) civil service.

7. On a scale of 1 (lowest) to 10 (highest), I would rate my over-all investment experience (actually investing) as _____.

   7(a). I have invested in stocks. ( ) Yes ( ) No

   7(b). I have invested in individual bonds. ( ) Yes ( ) No

   7(c). I have invested in mutual funds. ( ) Yes ( ) No

   7(d). I have invested in options or futures. ( ) Yes ( ) No

(continued)

My First Me Page *(continued)*

8. I currently earn $ _____ per year.

9. I am eligible for overtime pay at my job. ( ) Yes ( ) No

10. I plan on retiring from the work force in _____ years.

11. My risk tolerance from 1 (lowest) to 10 (highest) is _____.

12. I have other major expenses such as a mortgage, credit card debt, or saving for a home or my children(s)' college education. ( ) Yes ( ) No

13. I have life insurance. ( ) Yes ( ) No

14. I'm over 55 and I have long-term care insurance.
    ( ) Yes ( ) No

15. I currently have a financial plan of action for my retirement.
    ( ) Yes ( ) No

16. I have a comprehensive financial plan in place for all my finances. ( ) Yes ( ) No

You will notice that some questions on the Me Page ask about your investment experience and risk tolerance. Hold off filling these out until we have gone through the sections on these topics.

Your Risk Tolerance: It's Not a "Mind" Test; It's a "Tummy" Test

You may have the highest risk job in the world, but that doesn't mean you want to be or should be a high-risk investor. This is a critical self-test so let's take it one step at a time. Before we even start talking about risk tolerance, please remember one thing: It is your personal risk tolerance—not your neighbor's, or your coworker's, or your Cousin Horace in Duluth's risk tolerance. Your portfolio should be as individual as you are.

The following are some general rules. They are not set in stone. Simply use them as guideposts and adjust them to meet your needs.

The Age Test: How Old Are You?

A general rule in planning retirement asset allocations is to start with your age. Your age can help determine what percentage of your investments to allocate for aggressive investments and what percentage to reserve for more conservative ones. Your age is generally the percentage of your investments that should be conservative. For example, if you are 55 years old, then 55 percent of your investments should be made conservatively. Subtract your age from 100 (if you're over 100, then just use 100) and use this number as the percentage of your investments which can be more aggressive. Once you have this number, you can fine tune your portfolio by considering these other factors.

How Much Experience Do You Have Investing?

I have met a wide variety of individuals who work for state and local governments across the country. Some of these folks were former stock brokers and financial advisors for years before they decided to devote themselves to government service. However, many others have very little experience with investing and often entrusted the care of their retirement funds to a spouse, a parent, or a dartboard on their wall they nicknamed "Lucky." In short, everyone reading this book has a different amount of investing experience. And like when you start to learn how to swim, you should begin in the shallow end and gradually move your way toward deeper water.

What does that mean? It means that if you are in your early 20s and you haven't invested before or even if you are in your 60s or 70s and someone else took care of this aspect of your life, proceed with caution as you start to take control of your retirement funds. Often, a young participant may be strongly encouraged by a well-meaning representative who says, "Be as aggressive as you can! You have plenty of time."

In theory, this is a good way to invest because these individuals will generally have longer time horizons. So, what is a time horizon?

Time Horizons

A time horizon is the length of time you have until you can either begin withdrawing money or when you anticipate you will need to start drawing on the money. These may be two very different numbers, particularly for participants who have other sources of income such as rental property.

In the case of the young government employee, it would appear he should take on super high risk. In most cases, this is actually a huge mistake. Let me explain why.

Assume that Richard, a 25-year-old investor, begins contributing $5,000 a year into his retirement and then stops after 10 years. Jane starts her retirement savings at age 35 and starts contributing her $5,000 for the next 30 years. If both Richard and Jane get an 8 percent return, who will have accumulated the most money when each of them retires 30 years after they began contributing?

You would think Jane would have accumulated far more than Richard because she was contributing $5,000 a year for those 30 years. In fact, she comes out with $660,668, assuming annual compounding. But it is Richard who is the winner with $850,150 as his nest egg. It pays to start early!

Younger investors and those without investment experience should start off slowly! If you are a part of this group and you hit a bad bump early on you may decide to jump ship because you are so unhappy with the way things are going! You may start contributing again years later but, as you can see from the above scenario, you will never get the time back. It's far better to start out slowly and gradually increase your risk tolerance as you get more comfortable with investing.

SOUNDS LIKE A PLAN. *Danny is a single 24-year old firefighter with no children, working for a medium-sized city, who has little experience investing in the stock market.*

He wants to make a lot of money soon so that he can retire as quickly as possible—but he also has experienced savings only through his bank account, where his account balance never had the chance to decrease in value, unless he made a withdrawal.

What should he consider when creating his retirement strategy?

Danny has the advantage of youth. As a firefighter with generally a shorter time horizon until retirement, he should consider contributing as much as possible into his deferred compensation (457) plan, particularly because he is single and does not have to save for college education of children.

The flip side of Danny's situation is that he has no experience with investments that may lose value, while at the same time he wants to become aggressive. If Danny encounters a bad market, he may be inclined to scrap saving for retirement all together. Therefore he needs to downwardly adjust his risk tolerance early on until he gets used to the gyrations of the markets.

What to Do When the Markets Look "Ominominous"?

Growing up in upstate New York, I was no stranger to bad weather! My dad used to look out of our kitchen window as my family sat down for dinner and comment as the skies darkened, "It looks 'ominominous' out there." Not just ominous or foreboding— but ominominous—kind of the way the skies looked in Kansas right before Dorothy was swept up and everything moved into living color in *The Wizard of Oz*. Now let's move from my kitchen table to the financial markets of today. After years of seemingly endless prosperity and soaring stock prices, things may not always be as bright on the investing horizon. In fact, as one of my wittiest clients has commented, "Sometimes you wonder if that light at the end of the tunnel isn't just an oncoming train!"

A big part of making sure your portfolio is correct for you is periodically reevaluating your risk tolerance, particularly when the markets look ominominous. If your portfolio is keeping you up at night or causing you any kind of emotional unrest, you do not have the right portfolio and/or risk tolerance. It is easy to say that you are an aggressive investor when the markets are all performing well. But it's all right to realize that maybe you aren't as aggressive when things don't look so upbeat. The most important thing is that you are comfortable with your portfolio and, of course, that it performs as well as possible given your individual risk tolerance.

SOUNDS LIKE A PLAN. *Kristal is a 39-year old single mom without any alimony or child support, working for Human Resources at a small municipality, who put all of her retirement account savings into fast-growing stocks, and has watched her account sky rocket and then more recently lose substantial value. She is afraid to move her money because she knows that she cannot time the market, but she doesn't want to just sit back and keep watching her retirement nest egg shrink with each passing quarterly statement. Lately, she has started to lose sleep about her prospects for retiring, but she doesn't know what to do.*

What should Kristal consider for her retirement strategy?

One of the most important considerations that anyone investing in the stock market should take into account is her or his comfort level in investing. Kristal may have several more years of investing time horizon, so she can technically hold out in a poor market. But she has expressed that her portfolio is literally making her lose sleep at night. It is time for a change!

Kristal should consider moving at least part of her retirement account(s) into the Guaranteed Interest Account or CDs. This way, no matter what happens with the market, she will know that the assets in these ac-counts will keep growing and never lose value. Many of us are aggressive in-vestors in strong markets, who later realize we were more moderate or even conservative when we are faced with continued bad markets. It is important to recognize this and use it as an opportunity to re-evaluate the portfolio and redirect it in a way that makes us feel better so we can divert our atten-tions to other parts of our lives. For example, Kristal is the sole support for her family, so she has these added pressures. She should reduce the risk in her portfolio to the level where she feels more comfortable.

Building Your Pyramid: Diversification

Whenever I sit down with a government employee regarding his retirement plan, I first try to understand and gather all of the information that he has compiled regarding time horizons, investment experience, and risk tolerance. After that, it is time to figure out how he is best served. I find that the best way to visualize a person's asset allocation (and by assets I simply mean the money in your plan) is to draw a pyramid.

At the bottom of your pyramid, depending on your age, should be a layer of more conservative investments such as a guaranteed interest account, bonds, or if interest rates are favorable, money market. As you go further up the pyramid, you will want to have your core investments that are more aggressive than the bottom of the pyramid, but are well within your individual risk tolerance. There is definitely strength in numbers, meaning you should try not to put all of your money in one asset class such as large capitalization growth stock mutual funds or small capitalization value stock mutual funds. Over time, a more diversified portfolio has a better chance of outperforming a concentrated one. How does that work?

Imagine that the table you are sitting at right now is covered with empty glasses. Now imagine further that there is a little cloud over your head (on bad days that may not be so hard to imagine!). Over time, the cloud will drop rain into the glasses on your table. Not all of the glasses will get water each time. Sometimes, the rain will accumulate only in the glasses at the far end of the table while the rest don't even receive a drop of water. But over the long term, rain will accumulate in all of those glasses.

The glasses represent the different asset classes of your investments such as international; domestic; small-, large-, medium-sized stocks; and bonds. The rain is money. Sometimes when the markets are "ominominous," as we discussed before, it may feel like somebody drilled holes in all of your glasses through the bottom of your table. But other times the water will pour into your glasses. It's just important to have enough glasses out there to catch the rain when it comes.

A CAPITAL IDEA. If you are closer to retirement, you may want to have fewer asset classes. If you have an immediate need for your money, you may want to have only one, such as a GIA. Those with higher risk tolerances, longer time horizons, and more investment experience may wish to add more risk to the bottom tier of assets in their pyramids, though still keeping the risk lower than at the top of their pyramids.

THE BOTTOM LINE. The name of the game in regard to investing your government retirement portfolio is diversification. You do not want to keep all of your eggs (or in this case assets) in one basket unless you have an immediate need for your money. If that is the case, you should keep your money in very conservative investments such as in a GIA or a money market. Periodically, you should be revisiting your portfolio to make sure that everything inside is performing as well as their asset classes should be, taking into consideration your individual risk tolerance.

A CAPITAL IDEA. When the markets are rocky, the temptation is to put all of your retirement savings into guaranteed accounts. As we've discussed, this may be a good idea for part of your or even all of your retirement savings, depending on your individual risk tolerance and time horizon. But what if you have a longer time horizon and you are comfortable taking on more risk? How much will you sacrifice by just going into a stable account averaging approximately 5 percent versus a diversified portfolio with guaranteed interest account, stocks, and bond funds, if it averages 8 percent?

For illustration purposes, and assuming an investment at the beginning of the year of $10,000 for 30 years, at 5 percent you would save $732,488. However, had you gone with a diversified portfolio that had averaged 8 percent you would have ended up with $1,321,335.

INSURANCE: PLANNING
FOR THE UNEXPECTED

Most of us have had some dealings with insurance, whether it has been to buy car insurance, homeowners insurance, or life insurance. But what exactly is insurance, and what are the best and most cost-effective ways to purchase it? Finally, how does it fit within your government retirement plan of action?

HOW DOES IT WORK? Insurance: The Time Machine Substitution. *The easiest way to understand insurance is to think of it as your ability to get into a time machine and put everything that was damaged back to its original condition. Unfortunately, the money insurance can provide won't replace everything you may have lost. If you lose your ability to work, or a loved one, or even your own life, the insurance money will be a pale substitute for the things you would like to replace. Although no one ever wants bad things to happen, we pay insurance premiums to ensure that our families would be financially protected if anything ever did occur.*

UNCLE SAM'S CUT. *Because the purpose of insurance money is for replacement of a loss, it is not considered income. Therefore, there are generally no taxes on insurance money that compensates you for a loss.*

Types of Insurance You May Need

There are many types of insurance designed to cover you for the loss of anything valuable to your and/or your loved ones. An important strategy is to periodically review your policies to make sure that they are competitive in pricing and that they actually cover what you want them to insure.

A CAPITAL IDEA. Property Insurance. *Property insurance is just what it sounds like. It is insurance that covers your property be it your home or personal belongings. Many of us will move several times in our lives and therefore it is important to make sure that our insurance policies are up* to date and cover losses we wish covered. For example, if you are moving from a condominium to a single-family house you will want to make certain that your policy covers the new dwelling. As you get in the habit of annually reviewing your retirement plan of action it is a good idea to review your insurance policies at this time too.

Life Insurance

HOW DOES IT WORK? How many ads have you seen on television with a man and his wife playing with a child? They need some sort of life insurance in the event that one of them was accidentally killed. After all, what would happen to that beautiful child if one of the parents was no longer there? Well, none of us really likes to think about our own mortality. But what's the best way for you to protect those around you in the event you that you become the dearly departed?

A CAPITAL IDEA. Term life insurance. Those TV ads with the unbelievably low premiums or period payments for large amounts of insurance coverage are generally for term insurance. But what does term mean? It means that you are covered for the loss of your life for a period of years or a "term." There is no investment value in the insurance you are purchasing and if you unfortunately die after the term is over, your beneficiaries will get nothing. In essence, you are gambling that you might pass away during the term in which you are insured. Insurance companies are also gambling that if you are young and healthy (which they will verify), you are going to live long past the term and they can use the premiums you pay while never having to pay out any insurance money to you.

Whole life insurance. *This insurance encompasses term life insurance packaged with a product that gives you a cash value. In the event that you do not die, you still will receive some monetary benefit from the policy. As you may guess, whole life policies are more expensive than term life insurance policies.*

Start with your government employer's group plan. *Government employees are often best served by investigating whether your government employer offers group life insurance. This is often the most cost-effective way of obtaining basic life insurance coverage because you are using the economy of scale of the entire government employer to bring down your insurance premiums.*

Disability Insurance

More detail on disability insurance can be found in Chapter 8, but this will give you a basic overview of how it works. Additional discussion of what happens if you are disabled is also addressed in Chapter 8.

HOW DOES IT WORK? *Disability insurance covers you for the loss of your ability to work. It is considered a rather expensive form of insurance. What this insurance is designed to do is to replace the stream of income you may lose in the event that you cannot perform your job.*

A CAPITAL IDEA. *The most important aspects of disability insurance are the elimination period—the period of time until the disability benefits actually start to kick in—and whether it covers you for the loss of your own occupation or any occupation. Obviously, disability insurance for the loss of your own occupation is generally more expensive.*

As is the case with life insurance, you may find better deals on disability insurance through your government employer or through your trade unions. This is one type of insurance about which you may want to consult with an insurance broker or specialist to see if you qualify for it and if they can tailor it more to your individual needs.

THE BOTTOM LINE. When creating your government retirement plan you need to also look at your current insurance needs. You should review these policies annually to make sure that they cover everything that they are supposed to be insuring, particularly if you have recently moved. Examine what options your government employer offers for group life insurance. This may be a more cost-effective alternative for your basic life insurance needs.

CHAPTER 3

YOUR GOVERNMENT PENSION

The Cornerstone of Your Retirement

Y ou may not be able to directly control how your assets in your pension are invested, but that doesn't mean you shouldn't keep up with and maximize this very important part of your retirement strategy!

Now that we've laid the foundation for the raw materials that are inside your government retirement plan, we will move onto the actual plans themselves. The cornerstone of most government employees' retirement plans is their pension. Whereas other retirement plans such as deferred compensation (403(b)s and 457s and individual retirement accounts (IRAs) are often elective, if you stick with your government employer long enough to vest, you will generally end up with a government pension.

PENSION PLANS: ARE THEY DEFINED BENEFIT OR DEFINED CONTRIBUTION?

The two primary categories of retirement plans are defined benefit and defined contribution plans. I will discuss defined contribution plans in greater detail in the next chapter when I go over 457 and 403(b)deferred compensation plans. This chapter will delve into defined benefit plans, which you probably know simply as your pension.

HOW DOES IT WORK? *When you signed on to work for the government, you must have heard some coworkers say that the retirement benefits you will receive are a huge incentive. These people were referring in large part to your pension plan. There are a wide variety of pension plans in municipalities across the United States, but I am going to discuss the elements that are common to each. In its most basic form, a pension plan is a retirement savings mechanism that grants you a certain amount of money each year or a defined benefit after you reach an eligible retirement age depending on how long you work for the government. In a true defined benefit plan, the money used to fund your pension is contributed by your government employer.*

Although there was speculation that the Enron stock collapse and the problems with Worldcom in 2002 would impact some pension plans, none of them have indicated that they will have any difficulties making their pension payments. Unlike your deferred compensation or other retirement savings vehicles that we discuss later, your pension is not an individual account that will vary from worker to worker.

If you work for ten years for the same government entity and your coworker works in the same job for those ten years and makes the same salary as you and elects the same pension option as you, both of you will re-ceive the same pension payments when you retire. Of course, those are a lot of ifs. But unlike deferred compensation plans where often you control how your money is invested, pension plan funds are run for you.

A CAPITAL IDEA. Reciprocity between Some Government Pension Plans. There is more to your government pension than meets the eye. Not only should you know at what age your pension plan vests, but you need to know whether or not you have reciprocity between plans. What is reciprocity? Simply put, it means that even if your current government employer does not use the same pension provider as your for-mer government employer (particularly for different defined benefit pen-sion providers in the same state), you may be able to combine the two plans which can save you administrative hassles when you ultimately take your pension.

PUBLIC WORKING KNOWLEDGE. Government pension plans often are humongous funds, which are invested through the advice of consultants, professional money managers, and committees. Just to give you an idea how large these funds can get, here are the three largest pen-sion funds in the United States from both the private and public sectors. As you can see, all three are government pension funds.

- California Public Employees. *Total Assets: $143,887,000,000 of which $143,700,000,000 are defined benefit funds and $187,000,000 are defined contribution funds.*

- New York State Common Retirement Fund. *Total Assets: $106,091,000,000 all of which are defined benefit funds.*

- California State Teachers. *Total Assets: $95,553,000,000 of which $95,500,000,000 are defined benefit funds and $53,000,000 are defined contribution funds.*

(Source: Pension & Investments, *"The P&I 1000: Our Annual Look at the Largest Pension Funds" (Chicago: Crain Communications), January 21, 2002, pps, 12, 52.)*

How Is My Defined Benefit Money Invested?

Good question. Actually this is something that most state and local government employees probably do not spend much time pondering. A few employees may assume that their money is tucked away in some sort of interest-paying nest egg. More sophisticated investors may figure that these big pension funds with money to burn may be buying stocks and bonds for their funds. In fact, it is a bit more complicated than that. In fact, most government pension plans rely on teams of pension consultants who among other things evaluate the performance of their investments through such means as asset allocation and asset liability studies. These gigantic pension funds are often hiring professional money managers, some of which have familiar names such as Vanguard and Putnam. Many government pension plans are investing in a number of different areas you might not have assumed such as venture capital investments for start-up companies.

PUBLIC WORKING KNOWLEDGE. *Did you realize that your defined benefit government pension dollars may be invested in growth opportunities such as venture capital? The following are defined benefit government pensions which have the highest amount of assets invested in venture capital:*

- Pennsylvania School Employees. *$2,103,000,000 invested in venture capital.*

- Minnesota State Board of Investment. *$1,784,000,000 invested in venture capital.*

- California State Teachers. *$706,000,000 invested in venture capital.*

(Source: Pension & Investments, *"The Top 200 Funds with Defined Benefits Assets in Venture Capital" (Chicago: Crain Communications), January 21, 2002, p. 50.)*

My Government Pension: Smart Questions to Ask

- *When will I vest in my government defined benefit pension?* This question will help you determine how many years you have to work in your government job before you are entitled to your pension.

- *What percentage of my salary do I get in my pension for each year that I am employed at my government job?* If you receive 2 percent of your government salary for each year of the five years that you work in your government job, you will receive 10 percent of your salary when you retire.

- *How is my salary determined when calculating the final amount of my salary of which I will receive a percentage for my pension?* This will help you determine which years' salary figures are used to compute the wage on which your annual pension will be based. For example, does your pension look at the last three years in which you were employed and average these years to determine your salary? Or does the pension plan take your highest year of salary and determine your percentage pay out based on that highest year? This difference in computation can translate into thousands of dollars more or less in pension income when you are creating your government retirement plan.

- *At what age can I begin drawing my pension benefits assuming that I am fully vested in my pension plan and I am not disabled?* If your government employer allows you to begin drawing your pension at 50 years old, for example, it would mean that if you are fully vested with your government employer you would be able to get the determined percentage of your final salary as your annual pension income once you have departed service and are 50 years of age or older.

HOW DOES IT WORK? How Much Is in My Pension? *You should be receiving statements at least annually from your pension provider informing you how much money you have vested in your government pension plan. Remember, you can take the money that is vested out of your pension, but if you do that prematurely you will not receive any pension income once you have retired.*

How Your Government Pension Changes under the New Tax Laws

Buying Back Pension Credits Using Your Deferred Compensation

Under the Economic Growth and Tax Reconciliation Relief Act of 2001 (EGTRRA) you are permitted to buy back pension credits which increase the amount of money you would receive each year from your pension by using your 457 or 403(b) deferred compensation plan. Generally, pension plans will allow you buy back credits from the time you were a fully benefited, full-time employee. In essence, if you decided to pull money out of your pension, you may then use your 457 or 403(b) funds to pay into your pension plan.

PUBLIC WORKING KNOWLEDGE. *The Public Employee's Retirement Association of Colorado, with $27.6 billion in assets, has been experiencing phenomenal demand for purchasing service credits for their defined benefit pension plan by employees who, starting on January 1, 2002, were able to buy back service credits using their 403(b), 457 plan, and IRAs. Officials in Colorado anticipated a 50 percent increase in purchase agreements to buy service credits in their defined benefit plan, but the number of these agreements has virtually tripled from 165 in February 2001 to 542 in February 2002.*

(Source: Pension & Investments, *"Colorado Experiencing A Run On Service Credits." (Chicago: Crain Communications), April 15, 2002, p. 27.)*

UNCLE SAM'S CUT. *You do not have to pay taxes on the money being transferred into your pension plan to buy back credits. However, you should check with your government employer to make sure your pension allows for this.*

You Move from Job to Job: What Happens to Your Pension?

As long as your pension has vested you will be eligible to draw the amount of your pension to which you are entitled based on the formula set out by your government entity. If you move from one job to another and your pension plans do not have reciprocity, such as if they are from two different state systems, you may actually have several separate pension plans to track.

You Are No Longer Married

A qualified domestic relations order (QDRO) needs to be set up by the party that does not have the pension. Then this party will place the QDRO on file with the government employer where the ex-spouse is employed. When the time comes for the pension to be paid out, the government employer will then make sure the appropriate amount of money goes to the ex-spouse.

Can You Access Your Pension Money Early?

You can take a distribution of your pension money as soon as you depart service from your current employer. However, if you withdraw the entire balance you will not be eligible for pension payments when you are in your retirement years. Additionally, the money you take out will often be reported as ordinary income and taxable in the year in which it is withdrawn. Unless you are in dire need of the money from your pension, it is advisable to leave your pension money in the plan. This money will provide you with the bedrock of your retirement plan. If you have a severe need for the money, you may be able to buy back service credits at a later time.

If you take a lump sum distribution, meaning withdrawing your entire pension balance, and you are younger than 59$\frac{1}{2}$ years of age, you will be subject to the 10 percent penalty imposed for the premature withdrawal from a qualified plan. However, if your government employer allows you take annuitized distributions or periodic pension payments, you will not face this penalty. One way to take the money out of your defined benefit plan after you depart service from your government employer, and avoid both taxes and penalties, is to roll your pension funds into an Individual Retirement Account (IRA). In most instances, unless you have to roll out of a defined benefit program because you have not had enough time or become vested in the program, you are better served by leaving your money in the program.

Under EGTRRA, the maximum amount of defined benefit payouts increases from $140,000 to $160,000 per year. For all but a few government employees, this new provision will not have a great impact on your annual pension.

The End (of Work) Is Near!

As you get closer to retirement, you will need to decide how you will elect to take your pension funds. This will depend on a large number of factors such as whether you are married or single. If you are married, does your spouse also have a government pension? Is there a greater chance that one spouse will outlive the other? (Remember: statistically women still outlive men in the United States.)

UNCLE SAM'S CUT. *How will you be taxed on your government pension plan? Your money will be taxed as ordinary income the year in which it is withdrawn. You also need to determine if you will be taxed by another state if you leave the state of residency where you were employed. For example, if you draw your pension and decide to move, it may cost you to leave your state to retire to another state.*

PUBLIC WORKING KNOWLEDGE. *State and Local Government Pension Plans around the Country: Will You Pay State Taxes If You Move and Become a Resident of This State?*

- Alabama. *You will not pay any state income taxes on your state and local government defined benefit pension if you retire in Alabama.*

- Alaska. *You will not pay any taxes on your state and local government defined benefit pension if you retire here.*

- Arizona. *If you move to Arizona, your state and local government pension will be taxed by the state.*

- Arkansas. *If you move to Arkansas, up to $6,000 of your state and local government pension will be state tax exempt.*

- California. *Out-of-state government pensions are fully taxed in California.*

- Colorado. *If you move to Colorado and are between 55 and 64 years of age, $20,000 of your state and local government pension is exempt from state taxes. If you are over 65 years old, $24,000 of your state and local government pension is tax exempt.*

- Connecticut. *Whether you have a state and local government pension from Connecticut or you move here from another state, your state and local government pension will be fully taxed by the state.*

- Delaware. *If you are 60 or over, $12,500 of your state and local government pension is exempt from state taxes.*

- District of Columbia. *All out-of-state state and local government pensions are fully taxed in D.C.*

- Florida. *Because there is no state income tax in Florida, your state and local government pension will not be taxed by the state.*

- Georgia. *If you have a Georgia pension or move there from out of state and you are 62 years or older, up to $14,000 of your state and local government pension is exempt from taxes to the extent that you have the pension income to qualify.*

- Hawaii. *If you move to Hawaii, your state and local government pension is exempt from state taxes.*

- Idaho. *If you choose to retire to Idaho, your state and local government pension will be fully taxed by the state.*

- Illinois. *All state and local government pensions are state tax exempt in Illinois.*

- Indiana. *Your out-of-state state and local government pension is fully taxable in Indiana.*

- Iowa. *If you move to Iowa, your state and local government pension is fully taxable. If you are over 55 years old or are disabled, $6,000 of your state and local government pension will be exempt if you are an individual; $12,000 will be tax exempt if you are married filing jointly.*

- Kansas. *Your Kansas state and local government pension is fully tax exempt; however, if you move here from another state, your out-of-state state and local government pension is fully taxable.*

- Kentucky. *If you move to Kentucky, up to $37,500 of your state and local government pension is state tax exempt.*

- Louisiana. *Out-of-state state and local government pensions have a tax exemption of $6,000 for individuals and $12,000 for joint filers, if you are over 65 years of age.*

- Maine. *Your state and local government pension will qualify for a $6,000 tax exemption if you move to Maine. However, this may be offset by Social Security.*

- Maryland. *If you move to Maryland, your out-of-state state and local government pension is fully taxable. However, if you are 65 years of age or older, or you or your spouse is totally disabled, you may be eligible for a $17,300 pension exclusion.*

- Massachusetts. *If you move to Massachusetts and the state from which your state and local government pension comes does not tax Massachusetts residents' state and local government pensions, then your pension is tax exempt. Otherwise, it is taxable by the state.*

- Michigan. *If you move to Michigan, your state and local government pension is tax exempt for single filers up to $36,090 and for joint filers up to $72,180.*

- Minnesota. *If you move to Minnesota, your state and local government pension is fully taxable.*

- Mississippi. *If you move to Mississippi, your state and local government pension is state tax exempt, provided that you abide by your state's rules regarding your pension.*

- Missouri. *If you move to Missouri, your state and local government pension will be tax exempt for the first $6,000.*

- Montana. *If you move to Montana, your state and local government pension is exempt for $3,600; however, this exemption is reduced $2 for every $1 that your federal adjusted gross income exceeds $30,000 and completely phases out at $31,800 for individuals and $33,600 for married taxpayers filing jointly when both spouses have pension income.*

- Nebraska. *Your out-of-state state and local government pension is fully state taxed in Nebraska.*

- Nevada. *If you move to Nevada, your state and local government pension will not be taxed.*

- New Hampshire. *If you move to New Hampshire your state and local government pension will not be taxed.*

- New Jersey. *If you move to New Jersey and you are over 62 years of age, $9,375 of your state and local government pension will be exempt if you are an individual; $12,500 is exempt if you are filing jointly.*

- New Mexico. *If you move to New Mexico and you are 65 or older, up to $8,000 of your state and local government pension is tax exempt if your income is under $28,500 as an individual or $51,000 if you are married filing jointly.*

- New York. *If you move to New York and are 59½ years of age or older, $20,000 of your state and local government pension is tax exempt.*

- North Carolina. *If you move to North Carolina, $4,000 of your state and local government pension is tax exempt.*

- North Dakota. *If you move to North Dakota, your state and local government pension is fully state taxed.*

- Ohio. *If you move to Ohio, your state and local government pension is taxed subject to a $200 credit.*

- Oklahoma. *If you move to Oklahoma, your state and local government is tax exempt for the first $5,500 if you are at least 65 years of age and you meet the income limits of modified Oklahoma adjusted gross income. If you have an Oklahoma in-state state and local government pension then you are allowed a $5,500 tax exemption regardless.*

- Oregon. *If you move to Oregon, your state and local government pension will be taxed. However, if you were 62 or older on December 31, 2001 and you receive retirement income, you may be eligible for a retirement income credit, provided that you meet Oregon's criteria for this credit.*

- Pennsylvania. *If you move to Pennsylvania and are age 59½, your state and local government pension is tax exempt as long as you meet either your state's age or length or service requirement.*

- Rhode Island. *If you move to Rhode Island, your state and local government pension is fully state taxable.*

- South Carolina. *If you move to South Carolina, $3,000 of your state and local government pension is tax exempt if you are under age 65, and $10,000 is tax exempt at age 65.*

- South Dakota. *If you move to South Dakota, your state and local government pension will not be taxed.*

- Tennessee. *If you move to Tennessee, your state and local government pension will not be taxed.*

- Texas. *If you move to Texas, your state and local government pension will not be taxed.*

- Utah. *If you move to Utah and are 65 years old or older with income under $25,000 as an individual or $32,000 married filing jointly, you can exclude up to $7,500 of your Social Security and state and local government pension income.*

- Vermont. *If you move to Vermont, your state and local government pension is fully taxed.*

- Virginia. *If you move to Virginia, your state and local government pension is fully taxable. However, if you are 62 to 64 years old, $6,000 of your income will be tax exempt. If you are 65 or older, $12,000 of your income will be state tax exempt.*

- Washington. *If you move to Washington, your state and local government pension will not be taxed.*

- West Virginia. *If you move to West Virginia, your out-of-state state and local government pension is fully taxable. However, if you are 65 or older or are permanently disabled, you are allowed a modification of $8,000 for each person who is over 65 or permanently disabled.*

- Wisconsin. *If you move to Wisconsin, your state and local government pension is fully taxed.*

- Wyoming. *If you move to Wyoming, your state and local government pension will not be taxed.*

FOR YOUR REFERENCE. Pensions & Investments Magazine. *The bible for the direct contribution and direct benefit community. Very informative about trends and legislative changes.*

Pension Fund Excellence: Creating Value For Stakeholders *by Keith P. Ambachtsheer and D. Don Ezra, New York: John Wiley & Sons, 1998.*

You Are Now the Dearly Departed

What happens to your pension benefits after you die?

While you should check with your individual government employer to see if there are any variations, generally, your beneficiary(ies) will need to notify your pension provider of your death either by telephone or through the mail.

Most likely, they will be required to provide the following information about you:

- Your name

- Your Social Security number

- The date you passed away

- The name, address, and telephone number of your surviving spouse, your next of kin, or the person who has been designated to settle your estate

- The name, address, and telephone number of the person who is providing the notice of your death

Once your pension provider is notified, it will probably send out formal requests for documentation to the individual(s) named as your beneficiary, your next of kin, or the individual who let them know that you passed away.

Your beneficiary or next of kin will generally be required to produce the following information before they can be paid from your pension:

- A copy of your death certificate

- A marriage certificate, if your survivor is your spouse

- A completed claim form

- Letters of administration or letters of testamentary for cases involving probated estates if the estate is to be paid

- A copy of your beneficiary's birth certificate, if your beneficiary is designated for a monthly allowance

Some pension providers also ask for copies of newspaper clippings reporting your death, such as obituaries.

SOUNDS LIKE A PLAN. *Lisa is a married, 57-year-old mother of two grown children, whose husband works in the private sector. She has worked for the county as a clerical worker for 20 years. However, she took a break from the county, and at that time she withdrew money from her pension. She has grown her deferred compensation (457) plan to $175,000. She wishes to retire within the next three years and she will need to take money out of her 457 as soon as she leaves her job.*

What should Lisa consider when planning her retirement strategy?

Lisa's major consideration is her current retirement time horizon, which is just three years away. She needs to make certain that if she and her husband need to access her deferred compensation (457) assets, they will be there for them. Therefore Lisa may consider downwardly adjusting her risk tolerance for these assets. Lisa should also consider using part of her 457 plan assets to buy back service credits for her defined benefit pension, if her pension plan allows this, because the money she withdraws from her

457 as a government worker will not be taxed by the IRS to buy back government pension credits.

My Second ME Page

Me, The Pensioner

1. My name is _____.

2. My current government employer is _____.

3. I am eligible for a pension. ( ) Yes ( ) No

4. My pension provider is _____.

5. I will be vested in my pension on _____.

6. I am vested in my pension. ( ) Yes ( ) No

7. Currently, I draw _____ from my pension annually.

8. I have other pension plans for other government /nongovernment employers. ( ) Yes ( ) No

   a. Do I have reciprocity with any of these plans with my current plan? ( ) Yes ( ) No

b. Did I vest in each of these plans? ( ) Yes ( ) No

c. I am eligible to receive _____ from these pension plans annually. (If more than one plan add them up and TOTAL them.)

9. Is someone else eligible to take part of my pension money (e.g., ex-spouse)? ( ) Yes ( ) No

CHAPTER 4

GOVERNMENT DEFERRED COMPENSATION

Some Big Changes to Your 457 and 403(b) Plans in 2002

*T*his is one of the most exciting years in the history of the government deferred compensation plan! In January 2002, the Economic Growth and Tax Reconciliation Relief Act of 2001 (EGTRRA), which was signed into law by President Bush on June 7, 2001, went into effect. All provisions of EGTRRA, which brings sweeping changes for your government retirement plan will end on December 31, 2010, in what is called a "Sunset Provision." This year has been marked with uprisings and intrigue as to whether several states would adopt EGTRRA or not.

But before we get into all that, let's figure out what 457s and 403(b)s are and how you can best use them in your retirement plan. People unfamiliar with government employment benefits will often refer to government deferred compensation plans as 401(k)s. As a matter of fact, if you have searched bookstores and libraries for a book specifically about your state or local government retirement plan you may find virtually no help. With the passage of EGTRRA, many changes have occurred. There are far more freedoms—particularly for those in 457 plans—than ever before. But with freedom comes greater responsibility, so it is important to know a lot more than ever before. Let's begin with your third Me Page. Get out that pen! Hold off filling out the questions specifically about your plan until you finish reading this chapter.

My Third ME Page

My Government Deferred Compensation Plan(s)

1. My name is _____.

2. Today's date is _____.

3. I am ____ years old; I make $ _____ year; I currently defer
   $ _____/year into my deferred compensation plan.

4. I have $ _____ as my deferred compensation
   balance at my current government entity.

5. I have $ _____ in total (If you have separate
   balances list them and add them up!) including all my
   deferred compensation plans (401(k)s, 403(b)s, and 457s).

6. My government employer is _____.

7. My government employer has _____ deferred compensation plans.

8. Here are the names of my deferred compensation providers and what I like and don't like about each of them.

   a. _____

   b. _____

   c. _____

9. Has my government employer modified its plan document to allow for the new tax law changes? ( ) Yes ( ) No

   9a. If yes, which changes does my government employer allow? (E.g., I can now roll my IRA into my 457 or 403(b).)

   _____

   _____

10. Will I incur a "back end" surrender charge to switch providers? ( ) Yes ( ) No

11. I am ( ) appointed ( ) civil service ( ) not applicable

(continued)

My Third ME Page *(continued)*

12. On a scale of 1 (lowest) to 10 (highest), I would rate my over-all investment experience (actually investing) as _____ .

13. I currently earn $ _____ per year.

14. I am eligible for overtime pay at my job. ( ) Yes ( ) No

15. I plan on retiring from the work force in _____ years.

16. My investment risk tolerance from 1 (lowest) to 10 (highest) is _____ .

17. I have other major expenses such as a mortgage, credit card debt, or saving for a home or college education for my children. ( ) Yes ( ) No

GOVERNMENT DEFERRED COMPENSATION: PARTICIPATE BECAUSE THE PICTURE IS ALWAYS CHANGING

Forrest Gump's mother told him that life was like a box of chocolates. My mom told me that the picture is *always* changing, whether it was looking both ways before crossing the street or adjusting to new living conditions. No matter how many people you have advising you, it is ultimately up to you to get involved with your government retirement plan because as my mother

said, "The picture is *always* changing," and so are your retirement needs and the ways that exist to achieve them.

HOW DOES IT WORK? Deferred Compensation. *State and local
government deferred compensation, which includes sections 457 and
403(b) of the IRS code, is a retirement benefit. It allows you to defer money
from your paycheck before the government has taken out its tax bite. Inci-
dentally, it is that tax bite that the state governments were hungry for and
that is why many states resisted adopting the 2002 tax law changes which
granted bigger tax breaks and took tax dollars away from state tax coffers.*

*But remember: Once you begin contributing money to your deferred
compensation plan, it is not easy to take it out until you either depart service
from your current government employer, for 457 participants, or reach age
59½, for 403(b) participants regardless if you have left their government
employer. You may be able to withdraw money for a "hardship," but do not
count on that option being available to you.*

UNCLE SAM'S CUT. *In many instances, your overall taxes for the
year will be decreased because you can reduce your taxable income
by the amount you have contributed. Starting in 2002, you are able to defer
$11,000 or 100 percent of your eligible compensation, whichever amount is
lesser. This limit will increase $1,000 per year until 2006 at which time it will
be adjusted for inflation in increments of $500.*

*Under the new tax laws, there is an additional tax credit for contribu-
tions into your 457 or 403(b) up to $2,000 if your income is below:*

- *$50,000 for married couples filing jointly*
- *$37,500 for head of household*
- *$25,000 for single taxpayers*

403(b) and 457 Contributions

EGTRRA eliminates the requirement for you to coordinate your contributions between your 403(b) and 457 plans. In the pre-EGTRRA days, if you contributed to both a 403(b) and a 457 you could only contribute the maximum amount that the lesser plan (which was the 457) permitted. Because all plans now allow for equal maximums this coordination is no longer required between 403(b) and 457 plans. In fact, if you have both a 457 plan and a 401(k), you can contribute the maximum amounts allowed to each plan, as well.

Important for 403(b) participants: In the old days—meaning last year—you had to use a difficult calculation known as the maximum exclusion allowance (MEA). The MEA was used to potentially limit your contribution into your 403(b). Under EGTRRA, it no longer exists. Also any irrevocable election that was made in the past is no longer applicable under EGTRRA.

A CAPITAL IDEA. You should contribute as much as you can to your deferred compensation plan, but you should never feel "financially strapped" as a result of these contributions. If you are just starting out, you may want to ease your way into contributing by deferring the minimum amount allowed per pay period by your government employer. As you feel more comfortable contributing, you may then wish to contribute greater amounts. If you have one, check with your benefits specialist or director of human resources regarding how often you are permitted to change the amount of your deferred contributions per year.

Once you establish a deferred compensation account with your government employer, the money to fund your deferred compensation plan will automatically be deducted from each paycheck. Some plan participants like to "front load" or deduct a larger amount of money from paychecks early in the year so that they receive paychecks at the end of the year with no deferred compensation deductions.

Is Front Loading a Better Strategy?

You will put more money to work for you earlier on in the year. This is an advantage if your money is placed in investments which are performing well. Remember, you can never exceed your salary amount per pay period as a contribution into deferred compensation.

UNCLE SAM'S CUT. *When you withdraw all or part of your 457 or 403(b) funds, the money taken out will be reported to the IRS as ordinary income and will be taxable in the year in which it is withdrawn.*

The Hardship Rules: How to Withdraw Money from Your Deferred Compensation Account When Something Bad Happens to You

If you really need to withdraw money from your 457 or 403(b) before you are supposed to, you must satisfy the hardship rules of both your state or local government employer and the federal government. Under EGTRRA, if you satisfy these hardship requirements and take money out of your plan, you must wait six months until you can contribute to your plan again. Under the IRS regulations, an "unforeseeable emergency" is a severe financial hardship and includes:

- Loss of your property due to casualty

- Inability to meet your financial obligations due to a total disability

- $1,000 or more in uninsured medical expenses for yourself, your spouse, or a dependent

- A sudden or unexpected illness or injury from an accident to you or your dependent

- Inability to pay for funeral expenses for your spouse or a dependent

Some personal expenses which generally *do not* constitute a financial hardship include the following:

- Car purchase

- Home purchase

- Regular bills such as rent, mortgage, or credit cards

- Tax payments

- Educational expenses such as college

- Costs of elective surgery

When You Switch Jobs

Prior to EGTRRA, if you departed service from your government employer but got a similar job or "same desk" job at another employer you were not eligible to take a distribution. EGTRRA has repealed this rule.

What Happens to Your 457 or 403(b) If You Divorce?

403(b)s allow for QDROs to be attached to your plan in the event that you get divorced. The major change this year is that the qualified plan rules for QDROs now also apply to 457 plans regarding divorce distributions. Prior to EGTRRA, the use of QDROs was difficult to apply to 457s because they are nonqualified plans because you do not have to be 59½ and take your money out without incurring a 10 percent penalty. EGTRRA grants quasi-qualified status to 457 plans so that QDROs can be used in the event that the parties to a participant's marriage divorce.

Rolling Over a 403(b) or 457 Plan

Although 403(b)s have always been free to roll into IRAs, before this year, 457 plans were unable to move into IRAs because they are nonqualified plans. Neither 403(b)s or 457s could move into other plans except their own (such as a 457 rolling into another 457 plan) prior to this year.

That has all changed this year! Now you can roll your 457 not only into another government employer's 457 but also into a 403(b), a 401(k), or an IRA if allowed by the plan into which the funds would be rolled. Along these same lines, 403(b) participants can now roll their plans into 401(k)s, 457s, and IRAs assuming that these plans are set up to accept them.

To Roll or Not to Roll; That Is the Question

401(k) rollovers into IRAs create a huge market for financial service institutions. It is expected that government employees will be targeted with the same type of vigor once reserved for private sector employees. But should you roll your 457 or your 403(b) into an IRA after you depart service from your government employer? As any good financial advisor should tell you, yes and no.

When the Answer Would Be Yes

You may consider rolling your 457 or 403(b) plan if you have an outstanding financial advisor whom you trust will help you to grow your investments faster than you can do on your own using your current plan.

You may also consider rolling your 457 or 403(b) if your current plan is very limited and you can have far greater investment options by rolling into an IRA format.

You may also wish to roll into an IRA if your 457 provider will jettison your money out of your plan after a certain number of years and you wish to "stretch" your deferred monies using an IRA.

When the Answer Would Be No

If you have exceptional alternatives to choose from for deferred compensation including multiple providers and/or self-directed brokerage accounts (which we will discuss shortly), you may not want to move your money.

You may not want to incur additional commissions from buying load funds or no-load funds housed in a wrap fee structure, which adds a percentage fee on top of the fund's operating expenses charged each year. In many 457 plans, particularly those for participants in larger municipalities, there are no loads charged each and every time you move among funds.

For 457 participants, you don't want to move to a plan that cannot distinguish properly among qualified and nonqualified assets, meaning that if you rolled your 457 money into an IRA you have to wait until age 59½ to withdraw funds without incurring a penalty. For the most part, this should not be a problem thanks to computerization among providers.

Reverse Rolling: Yes, You Can Roll Your IRA into Your 403(b) or 457

Under the new tax law changes, you can actually roll your IRA into your current 403(b) or 457 plan. I will go into far more detail about IRAs in Chapter 5 when I discuss other retirement plans, but the kind of IRA you can roll in this case is the traditional IRA which was funded using pretax dollars as opposed to the Roth IRA which uses after-tax dollars. Should you ever consider "reverse rolling"? In certain instances, you may actually have a plan that is so well crafted with such a strong breadth of fund offerings and either low or no fees due to the economy of scale that this is actually more cost effective than buying loaded funds in your IRA and paying additional commissions to move in and out of them.

Important for 403(b) participants: Unlike the 457 participant, the 403(b) participant often does not have the tremendous framework of advisors that is offered to employees of state and city governments. For example, school districts generally stay far removed from dispensing advice regarding individual providers and often provide potential 403(b) participants, including school teachers, with an approved list of 403(b) providers from which they can choose their own. In one instance, I was advised that a government employer offered its 403(b) participants over 100 different providers among which to choose. This would be overwhelming for most of us.

Due to the larger number of offerings coupled with less guidance from your employer, you as a 403(b) participant may have a harder time selecting the best 403(b) plan for you. As you select among your 403(b) providers, use the information given below, but also realize that you may have fewer participants in your plan than government entities that only have 1, 2, or 3 deferred compensation providers. This dividing effect, where employees are spread across several plans, may make your overall fees less competitive than your 457 colleagues because the economy of scale may not warrant more cost-effective fees from providers. It pays at retirement time, in the form of a bigger nest egg, to choose carefully and to pay particular attention to fees.

EVALUATING YOUR DEFERRED COMPENSATION PLANS: SMART QUESTIONS TO ASK

Most government employers have deferred compensation plans in place. Unlike 401(k) plans, which only allow for one provider, 457s and 403(b)s permit multiple providers.

Increasingly, government entities have added more than one plan provider so that their employees have more choices, similar to being able to shop at more than one department store. If you only have one plan, you really can't choose among plans, but if you have more than one plan you should examine these plans very carefully.

SOUNDS LIKE A PLAN. *Mary is a 32-year-old public school teacher in a large district that provides its workers with a list of approved 403(b) providers. She has not started saving for retirement, but some of her fellow teachers have told her that she should get started. There are 75 names of approved companies and representatives on the list.*

What should Mary consider when planning her retirement strategy?

Mary should consider beginning her retirement savings as soon as possible, even if she only defers a relatively small amount such as $25 per pay period, so that she gets used to having money deducted from her paycheck. Because the money deducted is pretax, it will not seem like the full $25 is taken out anyway. One of Mary's biggest challenges is too much choice. When selecting among 403(b) companies and representatives, it is often a good idea to hear the comments of other individuals who have had both good and bad experiences with reps and their companies.

After that initial screening, it is also important to examine the structure of the plans, such as annuity or mutual fund based, while paying careful attention to the fees that each provider is charging. As Mary narrows her choices as a smart shopper, she should also talk with each rep and ask how he or she is compensated for working with her and what the policies are regarding educating 403(b) participants.

Differences among deferred compensation providers could take thousands of dollars out of your retirement nest egg.

I thought that statement might get your attention. Differences among your plans, particularly regarding fees, can add up to tens of thousands or even hundreds of thousands of dollars you may or may not see when you retire. So, look very closely at the following Smart Questions to ask prospective 457 or 403(b) plan providers.

Smart Question 1: What Are Your Fees?

Many deferred compensation plan participants have been amazed to discover that they have been paying fees that they never even realized existed. Recently, the Department of Labor has begun cracking down on this practice and is making sure that there is greater "transparency of fees." What does that mean to you? Full disclosure. The plan providers must let you know what they are charging you for their services. But what types of fees are there?

Types of Fees

The financial services industry has a lingo or vocabulary just like any other field. This industry groups fees as *asset-based, administrative,* and *operational expenses.* It sounds a lot more complicated than it really is.

The first two categories, asset-based fees and administrative fees, are charged by the provider—the company that actually provides the plan to the government entity. There are both *bundled plans* and *unbundled plans.*

In a bundled plan, the provider takes care of everything including record keeping and providing the investment options. Unbundled plans generally have two or more providers, each of which takes care of a separate area such as providing record keeping or providing the investments for the plan. The third type of fee, operational expenses, is charged by the mutual fund companies in whose funds you may invest when participating in a specific provider's plan.

Asset-Based Fees

Let's start with the good news first. Over the years, asset-based fees have been coming down. This is largely due to increased competition among providers for this type of business. The steady stream of income which flows in from government employees' contributions from their paychecks is becoming a more valued commodity. If asset-based fees are present, smaller municipalities generally, but not always, tend to have plans with higher fees. These fees are usually deducted from each participant's (that's your) account balance. They are also generally not graduated fees like income tax, but rather are a flat percentage which is assessed uniformly based on your assets in the mutual funds or other investments on which fees are assessed.

For example, if your asset-based fees are 25 basis points (a basis point is $1/100$ of 1 percent) then you are paying $1/4$ of 1 percent of your assets back to your provider. As you start out in the plan, this money will seem very small. But as your account balance grows, you will feel the pinch. If you have a choice between plans and there is a plan which does not charge an asset-based fee, look carefully at this option. Assuming your investments perform the same in both plans, you could save thousands of dollars by the time you retire.

Administrative Fees

You may find that you are being charged fees for the administration of your plan. As we discussed above, there are both bundled and unbundled plans. In a bundled plan, the provider does everything. It is the one that gives you your statement and your investments and provides the representative to help you when you have questions or problems.

When looking for which government plans the providers want to bid, they will consider many things, including the plan's quality of assets, which is the amount of money in the plan divided by the number of participants with account balances. Providers always want plans with higher average account balances or quality of assets and will reduce their fees to compete for them.

Providers will also examine the administrative costs associated with assuming the plan including record keeping costs, costs for staffing the help desk, and printing costs for paycheck stuffers and/or statements. These administrative costs are covered through administrative fees. Sometimes the municipality will pay for the fees and sometimes these fees will be assessed against the participant's balance. They are generally flat fees and do not depend on the account balance as do asset-based fees.

Thus, if there are two providers and one charges an asset-based fee and the other charges an administrative fee, participants with higher account balances may be better off with the administrative fee whereas participants with lower account balances or those just starting out may be better with the asset-based fee. Generally, there is fluidity within the plan so that you could switch providers if you desire.

Important for 403(b) participants: 403(b) participants who elect to set up individual brokerage accounts for their retirement plans will often encounter similar administrative fees which are charged by the brokerage firm for account maintenance and statement preparation. If you are selecting from a number of 403(b) options, shop around for the best administrative fees.

Operational Expenses

Most 457 and 403(b) plans are oriented toward guaranteed interest account or mutual fund based investing. In fact, 403(b) plans are mandated by law to *only* allow mutual funds as a form of investing. Remember mutual funds from Chapter 2? Each of these funds (load and no load alike) will charge you operating expenses. Please realize that these expenses are not being charged by the provider. Nor will you generally get a deal on operational expenses. They are charged by the fund companies themselves and will vary a great deal. It is important to understand that operational expenses are a key item looked at by the committee that selects the mutual funds for inclusion in your employer's plan. Unfortunately, 403(b) participants often do not have an entity selecting their funds so you may have to do this on your own or with a financial advisor.

Operational expenses for small cap funds that often have greater numbers of stock trades or international funds will generally have higher operational expenses than funds with fewer stock trades or domestic mutual funds. By the way, you can generally find out how much these operational expenses are via the Internet at Morningstar.com.

Now, how closely should you be looking at these expense ratios? Very closely. But do not use this as the sole criterion for either investment or plan selection. Weigh it along with the performance and the quality of the fund and its fund family.

Smart Question 2: How Can I Access My Account Once I Sign Up?

This is the Internet age. Examine how up-to-date your provider is and how easily you can access your account via Internet, telephone, and mail. Most larger providers and several boutique providers have state-of-the-art online capabilities, but it is always a smart idea to ask for a sample Web site address to find out just what you're getting into before you sign up.

Smart Question 3: How Many Investment Options Do You Have?

The number of investment options is becoming an increasingly important concern for participants as they realize that the greater chances for good asset allocation diversification may help to obtain better investment results over time. Of course, there does become a point at which you, the participant, may become overwhelmed and even confused if there are too many choices. This is a difficult balance to achieve.

Smart Question 4: Will There Be Any Back-End/Surrender Charges to Switch from My Current Provider?

This is one question many participants never think to ask. Every once in a while, a new provider is added to a government entity. You would assume that you could just move your money from the old provider to the new one, but then you see your statement and you're like, "What the fudge?" You find that a percentage of your assets suddenly vaporized as a back-end/surrender charge from your old provider. This is more likely to happen in cases where the old provider gave the participants a step-up or a percentage increase in their overall assets when it first came in. Be careful and don't forget to ask this question when you have multiple providers!

 SOUNDS LIKE A PLAN. *Greg is a 36-year-old nurse in a public hospital that offers its employees a 403(b) plan. He doesn't quite under-*

stand how the plan works and why he isn't better off just setting up a bro-kerage account on his own. He has also heard several of his fellow workers complain that the plan is very poor in its offerings and that the rep who services it is very inaccessible. He has talked with a number of coworkers about retirement, but he has consistently put off starting to save for retire-ment, but he would like to retire by age 60.

What should Greg consider when planning his retirement strategy?

Greg should consider that putting money into his 403(b) plan may be a great opportunity to save for his retirement because the money inside the ac-count will grow tax deferred. There is absolutely nothing wrong with setting a up a nonretirement or retail account for himself. However, the retail account will not have the powerful advantage of tax-deferral, which assuming equal investment performance may grow faster than an account on which he must pay taxes as the money is growing for such items as capital gains distributions from mutual funds. Greg is at a good age to consider creating his retirement plan of action. If his coworkers are correct that his current plan is limited in its investment options and his rep is not accessible, he may consider setting up a retirement plan with a brokerage house, even if he starts out by contributing $3,000 into an Individual Retirement Account. As Greg forms his plan of ac-tion, he will coordinate all of his retirement accounts together to produce the strongest retirement income generator to replace his income in 24 years.

Variable Annuities: Part Investment Product, Part Insurance Product

Both the 457 and 403(b) markets were targeted early on by very large insurance companies. In fact, up until 1974, all 403(b)s based on the law had to be annuity products. So, what is a vari-able annuity?

HOW DOES IT WORK? *Variable Annuity.* Think of an annuity like a giant egg. All the money you put inside it is tax deferred. Also, the investments contained within are often reported in annuity units that "scramble" the traditional share prices you would obtain from mutual funds contained inside. These same funds' prices contained outside of the annuity are reported in dollars making them somewhat more difficult to track in the newspaper or on Morningstar.com.

Some government employers have replaced their annuities for 457 plans across the country because they have preferred mutual fund plans for the reasons that follow. However, the annuity industry has begun adding additional features, such as enhanced death benefits, which has made them an attractive option. Unfortunately, the 403(b) market has lagged in this changeover. Therefore, if you are in a 403(b) or 457 variable annuity, you want to look very closely at the potential fees you may be charged for this product. In addition to the fees discussed above, you will probably encounter the following fees in the variable annuities used for 403(b)s and 457s which allow you to invest:

- Mortality and expense charges. *Because your variable annuity is by design an insurance product, it carries fees to ensure that you do not lose your principal.*

- Surrender charges. *You may actually pay substantially to leave an annuity 403(b) or 457 once you contribute your money. This also comes into play if and when you wish to move your 403(b) or 457 into another plan or an IRA.*

- Maintenance fees. *You may be charged either account fees or other fees to maintain your 403(b) variable annuity account.*

THE BOTTOM LINE. Annuities: The Pros and Cons. *When decid-ing whether to use an annuity based plan you should consider the fol-lowing pros and cons:*

Pros:

- *Some annuities may provide strong asset allocation models for the investment options contained within them. In these times of very turbulent markets, having a well-diversified portfolio is certainly a very big asset.*

- *Although this feature was not always present in some earlier annu-ity products geared towards the retirement plan market, some newer retirement plan annuities offer death benefits that may ac-tually restore the value of a portfolio to a higher level in the event that you pass away.*

- *Several annuity companies offer strong centralized help desks, should you have questions about the prices of your current funds contained with your annuity.*

Cons:

- *In a word: Fees. Annuities tend to have several fees, as discussed previously. If you believe you are getting something extra for these fees, such as a death benefit, then you may still be interested in choosing this form of retirement plan.*

- *Viewing investment prices inside annuities is not as easy as mutual fund based plans because these are reported in annuity units, which are not readily trackable by flipping your local newspaper open. Of course, you can call the annuity's help desk to find out share prices.*

- *Potential penalties. In certain instances, you may pay back end or surrender charges to leave an annuity before a certain number of years. Always find out how long your money is locked into this arrangement before saying yes to an annuity.*

Self-Directed Brokerage Account

Important for 457 participants: Proceed with caution! Remember that there are bull and bear markets. The bull market is categorized by soaring stock prices, whereas the bear market is a period of declining stock prices. In a bull market you may be able to move your money upward faster. But in a bear market you might find that what came up can go down even faster.

HOW DOES IT WORK? *As a direct result of the great bull market of the 1990s and early into 2000, many providers began self-directed brokerage accounts (a.k.a. SDBs). These accounts allow the participant to trade individual stocks and bonds as they would in a regular brokerage account but within their deferred compensation 457 plan. The advantage to these accounts is that there are not the same capital gains consequences in trading in these accounts that you would encounter in a nonretirement or retail brokerage account. So is this the right option for you?*

This comes back to what we discussed earlier regarding your individual risk tolerance and investment experience. In volatile markets, one who is not accustomed to the pendulum swinging downward faster may become panic stricken. Because they are often not diversified, individual stocks are generally far riskier than mutual funds. If you are absolutely determined to take advantage of this option, you may want to start out by using smaller amounts of money while keeping the remainder of your assets in the main plan invested in mutual funds and/or a guaranteed account. Keep this sobering mathematical fact in the back of your mind: If you lose one-half of the value of your portfolio, you must go up 100 percent to get back to where you were originally.

Important for 403(b) participants: Some 403(b) plans also have Self-Directed Brokerage options which are limited to mutual fund investments based on the limitations imposed on 403(b)s to only allow this type of investment vehicle. The one advantage to you may be a greater selection of mutual funds in which you may invest.

Smart Question 5: If I Sign Up, Is There Going to Be Someone There Who Can Help Me or Am I Going to Be Dropped Off by the Side of the Road?

Your deferred compensation representative can and should become one of your greatest allies in putting your government retirement plan together. Find out from talking with other employees if you will have access to this person. Also, find out about this person's qualifications including securities licensure and if he or she plans to hold individual and/or group meetings and what the frequency of these meetings will be. At a minimum, this person should be a human face for a large corporation who can help you navigate through a complex maze to get things solved. Hopefully, this person can also provide insight into what is happening currently in the stock market and the intricacies of his or her plan. Keep in mind that often these individuals are salespeople. They generally will not misrepresent facts, but they will present them in the light most favorable to their product.

A CAPITAL IDEA. *Have you ever heard the expression "getting your money's worth"? Your deferred compensation representative is the best example of this. You should find a rep (if possible) with whom you feel comfortable. Your rep should be knowledgeable about the investments in his or her plan. Additionally, many people will rely on their own financial advisor/broker to help guide them when investing in their deferred compensation plan. Don't be afraid to ask questions!*

A CAPITAL IDEA. Your Benefits Specialist: Tread Lightly but Ask. *As stated earlier, a benefits specialist may not be available to many of you who have 403(b)s. However, for those of you with 457s this person often does exist or his or her duties are performed by others with different titles. In a smaller government employer, your benefits specialist may not even be a person in a separate position, but may be the director of human resources or another employee that does this as part of his or her duties. Medium- to large-sized government employers often have a benefits specialist or teams of benefits specialists. For the most part, these individuals have a far more challenging job than most people realize. Not only do the benefits specialists have to keep up with what is happening with your retirement benefits, they often must be versed in the specifics of your health benefits and any other perks as well. In addition to interfacing with government employees, many times they are also working together with vendors or private sector providers for government employees. It's a rather demanding job!*

You should try to establish a friendly relationship with your benefits specialist and ask advice regarding the specific rules that your employer follows in areas such as how often are you permitted to change contribution amounts for your deferred compensation or what is the best way to contact your pension provider in the event that you have a question. Tread lightly but make sure that you ask as many questions as you need answered. Try to be systematic about your questions by making a list of them so that you get answers to all your questions.

Other Things to Consider with Your 457 and 403(b) Plans

Purchase of Service Credits Using Your 457 and 403(b) Plans

As of January 1, 2002, the funds held in your 457 or 403(b) plan can be transferred to purchase service credits for your government defined benefit or pension plan. However, this generally does not mean you can purchase service credits for time that you were not fully employed and fully benefited. Rather, it means that you can purchase service credits for the time when you worked and you withdrew pension money. Check with your benefits specialist or human resources department to determine if your pension plan permits this option.

UNCLE SAM'S CUT. *You will not pay any taxes on money transferred from your 457 to purchase service credits for your government defined benefit or pension plan.*

THE BOTTOM LINE. *If you need to purchase additional service credits and you have a deferred compensation balance, take advantage of this! Your deferred compensation plan is often more supplemental than your defined benefit pension, which is primary.*

The End (of Work) Is Near

What happens if you are getting close to retirement and you never participated in your deferred compensation plan at your government employer because either you weren't interested in the plan or you just couldn't afford it. Is it over for you? Not by a long shot! If you are three years away from retirement and/or 50 years of age or older you can elect to do a catch-up provision.

HOW DOES IT WORK? *The catch-up provisions for 457 and 403(b)s were complicated enough before EGTRRA, but now there are actually two catch-up provisions. As of January 1, 2002, if you're over 50 years old you can contribute an additional $1,000 per year into deferred compensation.* *This amount will increase in subsequent years as follows:*

2002	*$1,000*
2003	*$2,000*
2004	*$3,000*
2005	*$4,000*
2006	*$5,000*
2007–2010	*Adjusted for Inflation*

The Second Catch-Up Provision for 457s

Now, you can use the 457's second catch-up provision if you didn't contribute your full amount into deferred compensation while you were at your state or local government employer. You should check with your human resource or auditor's office to find out just how much you did contribute. Assuming you did not contribute, you may catch-up beginning three years prior to retirement by contributing twice the amount of the maximum allowable contribution for that year. For example, the maximum in 2002 is $11,000 so you will be able to contribute twice that amount or $22,000 for that year. As this amount steps up each year, you will be able to contribute double the amount for each year.

The very recently passed Job Creation and Worker Assistance Act of 2002 (JCWAA) modifies EGTRRA regarding a number of retirement plan issues. The major modification to state and local government deferred compensation plans under the JCWAA is simply clarification. You do not have the right to contribute under both catch-up provisions for your state and local government deferred compensation plan.

SOUNDS LIKE A PLAN. *Harriet has worked in public works for ten years as a part-time employee and ten years as a full-time employee. She is now 50 years old and would like to participate in her county's deferred compensation (457) plan. Harriet would like to retire in ten years, and she was eligible to vest in five years, and ultimately receive a defined benefit pension at 2 percent per year calculated by the average of the last three years of her salary. Her employer did not pay into Social Security, but she worked 40 quarters in the private sector prior to taking her county job.*

What should Harriet consider when planning her retirement strategy?

Harriet needs to play catch-up with her deferred compensation plan. Because Harriet is not in her last three years of employment with the county, she is not currently eligible for the three-year catch-up provision of deferred compensation, so she can only take advantage of the provision allowing her to contribute at an additional $1,000 per year because she is over 50 years old. Therefore, she should consider contributing $12,000 per year into *her county's 457 plan so that she is better able to reach her goals. Harriet's defined benefit pension which vested five years ago will make Harriet eligible for 2 percent by 20 years, or 40 percent of the average of her last three years of salary.*

Harriet will need to make up the 60 percent of her salary (or a reduced amount if she reduces her living expenses in retirement) she will not receive in pension. Because she will be retiring from a municipality that is not paying into Social Security, on the last day of her employment (assuming this does not change) she will have reduced Social Security benefits even though she is eligible for Social Security. Her deferred compensation plan should help to make up some of the money she will need to supplement her pension and Social Security.

The 15 Years of Service Catch-Up Provision for 403(b) Participants

Unlike the 457 catch-up provision that was modified by EGTRRA, the 403(b) second catch-up provision remained untouched. This provision is also mutually exclusive with the first catch-up provision meaning you cannot do both at the same time.

The guidelines for this provision state:

- Using this provision, you may make up the previous year's missed contributions into your 403(b) plan.

- You must have at least 15 years of service during which time you qualified to contribute to a 403(b) and you must have made average annual contributions of $3,000 or less.

- You can make contributions up to $3,000 with a $15,000 lifetime limit.

Taking Distributions When You Are Retired

Good news 457 participants: Those days of lock-step distribution hell are over!

In the old days, prior to 2002, if you were a 457 participant you had to sit down and plan out every last minute of your retirement before you decided how much you were going to take out of your 457 plan for your distribution. A distribution of money can be made using several different increments of time, but it is often monthly. Previously, you only had one chance to change the amount you set up for your distribution and if you miscalculated how much you needed you were headed straight for retirement hell. This is no longer an issue with the new tax laws.

As of this year, you can now defer your 457 distributions until the minimum required distribution age or $70\frac{1}{2}$ whichever is later.

Annuitizing 403(b) and 457 Distributions

Some of us like to have a steady stream of income for the rest of our lives similar to a defined benefit pension. Although annuities may be less cost-effective while you are employed than plans based on mutual funds, you may still opt to annuitize your plan when you retire. The trade off is higher fees and the risk that you may pass on before you run through your savings. Even mutual fund based retirement plan providers often offer an annuitzing option, so ask your rep if you want to elect this option.

What Happens to Your 457 or 403(b) after You Die?

Do you remember those forms you filled out on the first day when you signed up for deferred compensation with your government employer? Well, one of them should have been a beneficiary form. When you are playing the strings to your harp up in Heaven, you can rest assured that the individuals whose names are specified as either primary or secondary beneficiaries will be receiving the money contained in your deferred compensation plan.

FOR YOUR REFERENCE. *The following is a list of many of the major players in the government deferred compensation arena along with their postal and Web addresses.*

CitiStreet
Two Tower Center
PO Box 1063
East Brunswick, NJ 08816-1063
732-514-2000 or 800-537-6517
<welcomecitistreetconnect.com>

CitiStreet (For CalPERS)
Attention: CalPERS
Plan Administration
PO Box 9255
Boston, MA 02209-9255
800-260-0659
<www.calpers.ca.gov/benefits/defcomp/defcomp-program.htm>

Fidelity Investments (FITSCO)

PO Box 770002

Cincinnati, OH 45277

800-343-0860

<www.fidelity.com/atwork>

Great West Life & Annuity Insurance Company

PO Box 1700

Denver, CO 80201

800-537-2033 ext. 41308

<www.gwla.com>

Hartford Life Inc.

200 Hopmeadow Street

Simsbury, CT 06089

800-528-9009

<www.retire.hartfordlife.com>

ICMA Retirement Corporation

777 North Capitol Street NE

Washington, DC 20002

202-962-4600

<icmarc.org>

ING/AETNA Financial Services

151 Farmington Avenue

Hartford, CT 06156

<www.aetnafinancial.com/products_and_se>

Metropolitan Life Retirement Resources

Metropolitan Life Insurance Company

One Madison Avenue

New York, NY 10010

<www.metliferesources.com/MyRetirementAccount.html>

Nationwide Retirement Solutions (Formerly PEBSCO)

PO Box 182797

Columbus, OH 43218-2797

877-677-3678

<www.nrsforu.com>

Prudential Financial (Formerly Prudential Insurance Company of America)

30 Scranton Office Park

Scranton, PA 18507-1780

800-833-5761

<www.prudential.com>

T. Rowe Price Retirement Plan Services

PO Box 17215

Ownings Mills, MD 21297-1215

800-922-9945

CHAPTER 5

YOUR OTHER RETIREMENT PLANS

*Vehicles Able to Travel along Roads
That Never Even Existed a Year Ago*

Now that you understand the ins and outs of your defined benefit government pension and your 457 and/or 403(b) government deferred compensation plan, there are several other plans you need to learn about. Why? Well, many of you may have come from other employers in the private sector or you may be moving to another employer who will use other plans. Additionally, you can supplement and strengthen your retirement strategy through individual retirement accounts (IRAs). Just as the tax laws have changed regarding your primary government retirement plans, they have changed regarding these plans as well. In fact, it is rather fitting that retirement plans are often called vehicles because after the new tax law changes these "vehicles" can now travel along roads that before this year never existed.

PROFIT SHARING 401(A) PLAN FOR GOVERNMENT WORKERS

One of the more common plans you will find used by government employers or that is currently being considered for addition by government employers is a profit sharing plan which falls under section 401(a) of the IRS code. This plan may be used for a variety of reasons including creating a way for government employers to match their employees' contributions toward their retirement and as a means to create supplemental income in cases where the government employer does not pay into Social Security. The interplay between state and local government employees' pensions and potential reductions of Social Security benefits will be discussed in greater detail in Chapter 6.

THE BOTTOM LINE. 401(a) Plan. *A supplemental plan for certain groups of government employees, sometimes used as a substitute for Social Security.*

HOW DOES IT WORK? *401(a)s are also named profit sharing and money purchase plans. Under the old tax laws, individuals often used both profit sharing and money purchase plans because profit sharing plans have nondiscretionary contribution limits whereas money purchase plans grant total contribution freedom. These plans can be used as matching plans for deferred compensation or they can be used as substitutes for government employees whose employers do not pay into Social Security. Some of these plans will allow you, the participant, to invest your money through a variety of investment options, while other plans insist that you keep all of your investments in stable assets such as a guaranteed interest account.*

The trend has been toward allowing participants more flexibility in managing their own 401(a) assets.

A CAPITAL IDEA. *Important for 457 participants: Two main differences which used to exist between 401(a)s and your 457 deferred compensation plan is that a 401(a) is a qualified plan meaning that you will take a 10 percent penalty if you take the money out before age 59½ and you often can borrow against your 401(a), which is a very popular option for many government employees. Although you should check with your individual government employer, many government employers allow you to borrow the lesser of $50,000 or 50 percent of your 401(a) balance although some employers specify lower dollar maximums.*

Recently, the government has announced that it will be changing 457 plans to allow for loans similar to 401(a)s. Remember that even if this loan provision is allowed by the federal government, your state and local government employer must alter its plan document to permit this new feature.

401(a) Loan Provisions

If your government employer has a 401(a), you may have the ability to borrow against the money in this plan. You may take part of your plan assets out of your 401(a) account as a personal loan. Borrowing against your 401(a) is generally a pretty easy procedure. The only reason you may want to specify what the loan is for is because you may receive a longer payback period if the money is used for something such as the purchase of a home. Often your government employer will deduct your loan servicing payments right out of your paycheck, which can be very convenient for you.

UNCLE SAM'S CUT. *If you take money out as a loan from your 401(a), you will not have to pay taxes on the loan amount. However, remember you will be paying interest on the money you take out which is often set by your government employer and may be correlated to the prime rate. Additionally, when you do begin taking distributions from your 401(a) the money you take out will be reported as ordinary income in the year in which it is withdrawn.*

Should I Roll Over My 401(a)?

The issue of whether you should roll your 401(a) into an IRA or another plan is another decision you will have to make now that you have greater flexibility under the new tax laws. You cannot move your 401(a) into another plan if you have not departed service from your employer. Additionally, you should consult with your government employer as to whether they will be allowing either transfer of your 401(a) into its 403(b) or 457 plans and whether it will be allowing 401(a)s to accept rollovers from other retirement plans. What should you do if you have left your job and you are considering moving your 401(a)? Follow these three steps to determine if it is wise to move your 401(a) funds.

1. *Take a close look at how your 401(a) is invested and how it is performing taking into consideration market conditions.* If this retirement savings vehicle has been performing well considering market conditions, you may wish to check with your current provider to determine if you can stay in this plan. If this is an option, check to see if there are

any fees that your provider is charging for this service. Generally, if you are allowed to leave your plan with your current provider, you should be treated the same as any other 401(a) participant.

2. *If you have a new 401(a), examine your new investment options closely.* For administrative ease, you may wish to consolidate your plans. But if you have the option of leaving your plan with your current provider, you really want to take a careful look at the plan into which you are considering moving. Ask whether this new plan has the same breadth of investment options and try to determine the performances of these investments over one, three, five, and ten years.

3. *Check to see if you will be paying higher or lower fees with your new 401(a) provider.* As was discussed in evaluating 457 plans in Chapter 4, make a careful comparison between the plans to see which one charges asset-based fees or administrative fees. Sometimes you will find it much more cost-effective to stay with your old provider. Other times, this may be a great chance to cut back on fees with a new provider.

What to Do If Your New Government Employer Doesn't Have a 401(a)

First of all, you may have more options than you think with the recent tax law changes. If you are able to keep your 401(a) with your current provider; your current plan has low or no fees; and you are happy with your investment options, performance, and the guidance you are receiving regarding the account, you should probably stay put. However, if your loan balances are all paid off, you can also roll your 401(a) into an IRA this year under the new tax laws. IRAs will be discussed in greater detail later in this chapter, but you should know that there are a number of financial institutions that provide IRAs. The key is selecting the right financial institution and/or financial professional for your individual needs.

If you have a strong relationship with a financial advisor, you may wish to roll your 401(a) into an IRA. As we will discuss shortly, an IRA will generally provide you with greater flexibility than most 401(a) plans, particularly those which lack a self-directed brokerage account. If you are considering whether to go with a financial professional, take a look at the discussion on selecting and working with a financial advisor in Chapter 7.

401(k) PLANS: PRIVATE SECTOR PLANS USED OCCASIONALLY IN THE PUBLIC SECTOR

You may hear your 457 plan described by individuals unfamiliar with government deferred compensation plans as 401(k)s. This term has become generic to some for any plan that is used for defined contribution retirement savings. In Chapter 4, you learned the ins and outs of your 457 or 403(b) plan, which is your government defined contribution plan. Now, let's take a look at the 401(k).

HOW DOES IT WORK? *Although most government employers use 457 or 403(b) plans for their employees, some municipalities have been grandfathered in with 401(k) plans for their employees. 401(k) plans are more associated with the private sector and up until this year had a distinct advantage over the 457 or 403(b) in that you could contribute greater amounts in the 401(k) than you could in the 457 or 403 (b). Under EGTRRA, this advantage has been removed because all three plans now allow for a maximum $11,000 contribution per year. Many 401(k) employers offer the added benefit of contributing money toward their employees' 401(k)s often in the form of matching employee salary deferrals.*

A major distinction between 401(k) plans and 457s is that a 401(k) is qualified, meaning you cannot take your money out of the 401(k) until age 59½ without incurring a 10 percent penalty. With a 457, once you leave your municipality, you can take your money out without incurring any penalty. Also, 401(k)s generally only allow one provider whereas 457 and 403(b) plans allow multiple providers, which is often the case among state and local government employers.

So what happens if you roll your 401(k) into your 457 plan? You should keep strong documentation of all of your plans because your 401(k) funds rolled into your 457 will be treated separately for purposes of withdrawing them prior to 59½ years of age.

THE BOTTOM LINE. *You can't roll your 401(k) into your 457 in order to get rid of the early withdrawl penalty of qualified plans.*

When to Consider Rolling Over Your 401(k)

If you have a 401(k) from a former employer you should check the mutual fund and/or other investment selection present in your new plan. If you feel limited by both your 401(k) and your 403(b) or 457, you may wish to consider rolling it into an IRA in order to take advantage of the extensive investment offerings which can be used in this retirement account.

SOUNDS LIKE A PLAN. *Pete is a 48-year-old mass transit bus driver for a large municipality that does not pay into Social Security. He has worked in the private sector for several years prior to his current job and he is attempting to plan for his government retirement. Pete has a rather large IRA and a 401(k) from his former private sector employer that only has three mutual funds. His current municipality has three highly regarded 457 plans from which he may select.*

What should Pete consider when planning his retirement strategy?

Pete should consider the relative strengths and weaknesses of his past plan, his IRA account, and his potential 457. No matter what his decision, Pete should establish a 457 plan with his new employer by carefully examining fees, investment options, and the accessibility of his plans' representatives. If Pete is comfortable with his new plan, he may consider rolling his former 401(k) plan into his IRA or 457, because it had very limited investment options. Pete also has the ability to reverse roll his IRA into his 457 plan if his new municipality permits this.

Catch-Up Provisions for 401(k)s

If you are 50 years or older, you may catch up your contributions into your 401(k). These contributions do not count against the maximum elective deferral permitted for 401(k) plans. For example, in 2002, if you are 50 years old you can contribute $12,000, which includes the $11,000 maximum contribution and the $1,000 catch up. The following is a schedule of 401(k) catch ups:

Year	Contribution Maximum
2002	$1,000
2003	$2,000
2004	$3,000
2005	$4,000
2006	$5,000

INDIVIDUAL RETIREMENT ACCOUNTS (IRAS)

HOW DOES IT WORK? *You may have started an IRA long before coming to work for the government or while you have been working with the government. An individual retirement account is basically a means for you to tax defer money outside of your established defined contribution plan. There are two types of IRAs: traditional and Roth.*

A CAPITAL IDEA. *If you were to think of retirement savings plans as existing in a land of different vessels each of which has its own functions, the individual retirement account was for many years an individual vessel used to pull money out of your taxable income to set aside in an individual account with a bank or your broker. Then, with the introduction of the Roth IRA, this gigantic vessel suddenly was cloned and another container was created which serves the function of helping you augment your retirement savings in an often more flexible manner. But there are distinct differences between a traditional IRA and a Roth IRA.*

IRA Contribution Limits under the New Tax Law

The annual contribution limits for both traditional and Roth IRAs are as follows:

2002–2004	$3,000
2005–2007	$4,000
2008	$5,000
2009	Indexed in $500 multiples

The Traditional IRA

HOW DOES IT WORK? *The traditional IRA allows you to put aside money for your retirement in addition to your 457 or 403(b) plan. Whether you can deduct the money you put into this retirement savings vehicle is dependent upon a number of factors. Let's take a look at this type of retirement account on which millions of Americans rely.*

Anyone under age 70½ who works can open up a traditional IRA. Additionally, if you work and your spouse does not work, you may make contributions on behalf of your spouse. The money you put into this retirement vehicle can be placed in a wide range of investments including individual stocks, bonds, and mutual funds. This money will grow tax-deferred inside the IRA until you are ready to take it out.

Can I Open Up a Traditional IRA If I Already Have a 457 or 403(b) Plan?

Yes. Even if you are covered by your government employer-sponsored retirement plan, you can contribute up to the maximum contribution into your IRA each year.

UNCLE SAM'S CUT. *Even if you can contribute the maximum to your traditional IRA, the amount of your contribution that you can deduct from your income tax depends on your adjusted gross income if you are covered by an employer-sponsored retirement plan.*

Are You Covered by Your Government Employer's Sponsored Plan?

The easiest way to determine this is to take a look at your W-2 forms. If the "Retirement" box is checked on your W-2, the IRS will assume that you are covered by your government employer's sponsored plan.

THE BOTTOM LINE. *If you are not covered by your employer-sponsored retirement plan, the money that you contribute into you traditional IRA is deductible, no matter how high your adjusted gross income.*

Traditional IRA Deductability If You Are Covered by Your Government Employer-Sponsored Retirement Plan

Your contributions to the traditional IRA for your non-working spouse are tax deductible up to the maximum allowed contribution as long as you are married filing jointly and your joint income is $160,000 a year or less.

Single Taxpayers Covered by an Employer-Sponsored Plan

Adjusted Gross Income	Deductibility
Less than $34,000	Completely deductible
$34,000–$44,000	Partially deductible
Greater than $44,000	Not deductible

Married Taxpayers Covered by an Employer-Sponsored Plan

Adjusted Gross Income	Deductibility
Less than $54,000	Completely deductible
$54,000–$64,000	Partially deductible
Greater than $64,000	Not deductible

The End (of Work) Is Near: Traditional IRA Distributions

Once you reach $59\frac{1}{2}$ years of age you may take out as much money from your traditional IRA as you like without incurring a 10 percent penalty.

UNCLE SAM'S CUT. *All money that you withdraw from a traditional IRA is reported as ordinary income in the year in which it is withdrawn and as such it is subject to taxes.*

Minimum Distributions

When you reach age $70\frac{1}{2}$, you must begin taking withdrawals and set up a distribution method from your traditional IRA or you will face penalties.

You Are Now the Dearly Departed

When you establish your traditional IRA, you will be asked to complete a beneficiary form. These forms can be changed. However, you will often be required to obtain a spousal consent in the event that you wish to remove your spouse as your traditional IRA beneficiary.

The Roth IRA

The Roth IRA also allows you to set aside money for your retirement if your income level qualifies you. For 2002, you can put money into a Roth IRA if you meet the following criteria:

Single Taxpayers Eligible for Roth IRAs

Adjusted Gross Income	*Eligibility*
Less than $95,000	Can contribute full amount
$95,000–$110,000	Can contribute partially
Greater than $110,000	Cannot contribute to a Roth

Married Taxpayers Eligible for Roth IRAs

Adjusted Gross Income	*Eligibility*
Less than $150,000	Can contribute full amount
$150,000–$160,000	Can contribute partially
Greater than $160,000	Cannot contribute to a Roth

HOW DOES IT WORK? *Unlike the traditional IRA, Roth IRAs do not allow you to deduct the contribution from your income taxes. In return for this, the money housed inside this retirement account grows* *tax-deferred and when it is withdrawn you do not pay any income taxes on it.*

Choosing between the Traditional and the Roth IRA

If you qualify for both a Roth and a deductible traditional IRA and you expect that your tax rate will be much lower when you retire than it is now, you may prefer a traditional IRA.

If you qualify for both a Roth and a deductible traditional IRA and you expect that your tax rate will be much higher when you retire, then you may choose a Roth IRA.

Because Roth IRA contributions can be taken out at any time, if you anticipate needing your contribution money before age $59\frac{1}{2}$ and are able to contribute to a Roth, it is the better IRA choice for you.

If you are over age $70\frac{1}{2}$, still have earned income, and you qualify for a Roth IRA, you would want to contribute to a Roth—particularly because there is no mandatory distribution with a Roth IRA.

Can You Contribute to Both a Roth and Traditional IRA in the Same Year?

Yes, as long as you do not exceed the maximum contribution limit for that year. For example, if your adjusted gross income qualifies you for only a partial contribution to a Roth, you may set up a Roth IRA for that part and a traditional IRA for the remainder of the maximum allowed contribution. In 2002, if you were only able to contribute $1,000 into a Roth IRA, you could also contribute $2,000 into a traditional IRA in order to achieve the $3,000 maximum contribution.

Conversion between the Traditional and Roth IRA

The Roth IRA was created in 1997. At that time Congress gave owners of traditional IRAs the option of converting their current IRA into a Roth IRA. The table below defines the eligibility requirements for conversion.

If You Are a	With Modified AGI of $100,000 or Less	With Modified AGI of $100,000+
Single Taxpayer	May Convert	May Not Convert
Married Taxpayers Filing Jointly	May Convert	May Not Convert
Married Taxpayers Filing Individually	May Not Convert	May Not Convert

UNCLE SAM'S CUT. What Happens When You Convert from a Traditional IRA to a Roth? *If you convert from a traditional IRA to a Roth IRA, you will have to pay all applicable taxes in the year in which you convert. All deductible contributions from your traditional IRA will be taxed as ordinary income when you convert to the Roth. There are no 10 percent premature federal tax penalties even if you are under 59½. Additionally, you can do a partial Roth conversion.*

Reversing a Roth IRA Conversion

After you have decided that you want to convert from a traditional IRA to a Roth IRA you can reverse the conversion. You may wish to do this if one of the following has happened:

- The market value of your IRA portfolio has declined following the conversion. You want to reverse the conversion in order to avoid paying any taxes based on the relatively high valuations that existed in the portfolio at the time the IRA converted.

- Your adjusted gross income actually turned out to be higher than $100,000.

When Must You Do Your Roth Recharacterization?

You have until you tax filing, which includes extensions, in the year following your IRA conversion to make a recharacterization of your Roth back to a traditional IRA. If you do decide to recharacterize your Roth back to a traditional IRA, you cannot reconvert again to a Roth IRA in the same year.

You may not reconvert a traditional IRA back to a Roth IRA before the longer of either January 1 of the following tax year or 30 days after recharacterization takes place. Here are a couple of examples of how this works.

Let's assume that you convert to a Roth IRA in December 2002. Then you recharacterize back to a traditional IRA in January 2003. You can't reconvert back to a Roth IRA until January 1, 2004.

If you convert to a Roth IRA in June, and then recharacterize it back to a traditional IRA on December 15 of the same year, you can't reconvert back to a Roth until January 16 of the following year.

SIMPLE IRAs

HOW DOES IT WORK? *Savings incentive match plan for employees IRAs, or SIMPLE IRAs, are used by employers, including some government agencies, with 100 or fewer employees. Any employee who earned $5,000 or more during the last two years of employment and anticipates earning at least $5,000 during the current year is eligible to participate.*

How Much Can Be Contributed into a SIMPLE IRA Per Year?

The following table lists the contribution amounts for SIMPLE IRAs.

Year	Contribution Maximum
2002	$7,000
2003	$8,000
2004	$9,000
2005	$10,000
2006–2010	Indexed

Rolling Over SIMPLE IRAs

Traditional and Roth IRA contributions cannot be made into SIMPLE IRAs nor can traditional, Roth, or SEP IRAs be rolled over into SIMPLE IRAs. After you have participated in a SIMPLE IRA for two years, you may roll your SIMPLE IRA into other retirement plans including traditional and Roth IRAs, 401(k)s, 403(b)s, 457s, and 401(a)s.

THE BOTTOM LINE. *Unlike the traditional IRA which carries a 10 percent penalty for early withdrawal of money prior to age 59½, you must wait two years to withdraw money prematurely from a SIMPLE IRA or face 25 percent penalties. After the two years has elapsed, the penalty is 10 percent, the same as the traditional IRA's penalty for premature withdrawal.*

SIMPLE IRA Catch Up

Once you turn 50 years old, your plan may allow you to make a catch-up contribution into your SIMPLE IRA. This contribution does not count against your maximum elective deferral limit for SIMPLE IRAs. For example, in 2002 you would be permitted to contribute $7,500 into your SIMPLE IRA if you are over 50 years of age. The following is the catch-up contribution schedule for SIMPLE IRAs.

Year	Contribution maximum
2002	$ 500
2003	$1,000
2004	$1,500
2005	$2,000
2006	$2,500

SEP IRAs

HOW DOES IT WORK? *Simplified Employee Pension IRAs, or SEP IRAs, are among the retirement plans which have been most changed this year by the new tax laws. This retirement vehicle is designed for small business owners who desire tremendous flexibility in how much to contribute toward retirement each year.*

A CAPITAL IDEA. *Using the SEP IRA, self-employed individuals can contribute the lesser of 25 percent of their salary or $40,000 per year. A major advantage of SEP IRAs is that they are inexpensive to administer and have fewer complications than other plans. The contributions made into your SEP IRA are tax-deferred until they are withdrawn. Unlike SIMPLE IRAs, where participants must wait two years in order to avoid the heavy 25 percent penalty, SEP IRA participants do not have any waiting period. However, if you make a premature withdrawal prior to 59½, you will pay a 10 percent penalty.*

SOUNDS LIKE A PLAN. *Nina is a divorced, 51-year-old Assistant Attorney General for the State who is also a very entrepreneurial businesswoman. She often earns more income from her side business based out of her home than she does as an attorney for the state. Nina wants to maximize her government retirement strategy.*

What should Nina consider when planning her retirement strategy?

Nina should consider contributing as much as she can to her state deferred compensation plan to reduce her taxable income as an Assistant Attorney General. Because Nina is over 50 years old, she is also allowed to contribute an additional $1,000 into her deferred compensation plan for a total of $12,000 in 2002. Additionally, Nina should set up a SEP IRA for her business, which allows her to contribute the lesser of 25 percent of her income from the business or $40,000 per year. Establishing both retirement plans will maximize Nina's ability to get to her retirement goals faster.

Taking Money out of Your IRA before Age 59½ without Penalty

Normally, you will pay a 10 percent federal penalty on any money you take out of your IRA before the age of 59½. However, there are some ways that you can take money out of your IRA penalty-free.

- *Medical expenses.* You may withdraw money from your IRA without paying a penalty if you can demonstrate that it is for medical expenses that exceed 7.5 percent of your adjusted gross income.

- *Medical insurance.* If you become unemployed, you may be able to take money out of your IRA in order to pay for medical insurance without having to pay a penalty on that money.

- *Buying a home.* You have the ability of one lifetime withdrawal of $10,000 from your IRA, without incurring a penalty, to buy a new home. You have to use the money to buy a first home or a home that is bought at least two years after the sale of a previous home.

- *College costs.* You may deduct money penalty-free from your IRA for costs associated with college. These costs may include room and board, tuition, and books.

Rule 72(t)

Let's assume that you want to retire early. Great thought isn't it? Is there any way in which you can tap into your IRA with paying that nasty 10 percent penalty? Yes, and it is known as Rule 72(t).

HOW DOES IT WORK? *Rule 72(t) can be used for both traditional and Roth IRAs if you meet the IRS's conditions to the "T." The following conditions must be strictly met in order to take advantage of Rule 72(t):*

- *You have to take your distributions from whatever IRA(s) you choose in "substantially equal" periodic payments over the length of your life expectancy or over the length of the joint life expectancy of you and your designated beneficiary.*

- *You have to take these substantially equal distributions at least once each year.*

- *You cannot modify the distribution schedule you establish for taking these substantially equal payments other than for your disability or in the event that you die within five years of beginning distribution, or you reach age 59½ whichever date is later. Once you have reached the fifth year or age 59½, you can change your distribution amount or stop it.*

The Ways You Can Choose Your Periodic Payment under Rule 72(t)

There are three ways in which you can determine the periodic payments you will receive from your IRA under Rule 72(t): annuitization, amortization, and life expectancy.

1. *Annuitization method.* If you use this method, you will provide a consistent stream of income each year. It basically determines your payment by dividing your IRA balance by the number of years you are expected to receive payments.

2. *Amortization method.* Under this method you will spread out the principal evenly using your life expectancy or the joint life expectancy of you and your designated beneficiary. Like the annuitization method, this will also create a steady stream of income.

3. *Life expectancy method.* Just as the name states, this method bases your payment on your life expectancy or on the joint life expectancy of you and your designated beneficiary. This life expectancy number comes from the IRS life expectancy table. Unlike both annuitization and amortization, the payments under this method will begin smaller and increase over time. If you elect this method you will have to recalculate your distribution amount on the anniversary of your first distribution.

Using Your IRA(s) to Diversify Your Portfolio

Starting or contributing into your IRA has more benefits than just putting aside money into a tax-deferred nest egg. By placing your money into this vessel, you can actually diversify your portfolio by placing these investments in another strategy. For example, let's assume that your deferred compensation plan was invested in a primarily growth-oriented portfolio and you believe that this portfolio, which was hit hard in 2001, will come back strong if you give it time. You can shift or begin to make IRA contributions with a value approach to investing or change your focus from domestic investments to include more international investments in your portfolio.

My Fourth ME Page

My Other Retirement Account(s)

1. My name is _____.

2. Today's date is _____.

3. The other retirement plans where my money is invested are as follows:

   a. _____

   What annual fees am I paying in this plan? _____

   b. _____

   What annual fees am I paying in this plan? _____

4. My government employer is _____.

(continued)

My Fourth ME Page *(continued)*

5. The 457 or 403(b) plan(s) that are available to me include:

   _____.

6. I have set up an IRA account. ( ) Yes ( ) No

   a. If yes, my IRA's total balance is $_____.

7. I have a SEP or SIMPLE IRA. ( ) Yes ( ) No

   a. If yes, my IRA's total balance is $_____.

8. I have a 401(a) plan. ( ) Yes ( ) No

   a. If yes, do I have outstanding loans on this plan? ( ) Yes ( ) No

   b. If yes, these are the balances of the loans and the duration of the loans _____ _____.

CHAPTER 6

SOCIAL SECURITY

How Does It Fit into My Game Plan?

HOW DOES IT WORK? *Contrary to many younger investors' beliefs, Social Security has not been around since the beginning of time or even the beginning of this country. This part of your government retirement plan will kick in at different ages depending on when you were born. If you were born before 1938, your full retirement age is 65. As of 1983, the laws regarding Social Security were changed to gradually increase retirement age to 67 for those born in 1960 and after. As a state and local government employee, the aspect of Social Security most critical to you is whether your state or local government employer pays into it. If you worked for an employer that did not participate in Social Security, what are the consequences to your Social Security benefits for both you and your spouse and/or widow(er)?*

 A CAPITAL IDEA. *Everyone 25 years of age or older who has paid into Social Security receives an annual statement from Social Security*

giving you an estimate of how much money you can expect to receive from Social Security.

THE BOTTOM LINE. What Happens If Your Government Employer Doesn't Pay into Social Security? *If your employer doesn't pay into Social Security your Social Security retirement and disability benefits and those of your spouse may be reduced.*

THE WINDFALL ELIMINATION PROVISION AND YOU, THE GOVERNMENT EMPLOYEE

Section 218 of the Social Security Act provides Social Security benefits to state and local government employees. However, if you work for a government employer that does not pay into Social Security, the pension which you receive from that job may reduce your Social Security benefits. Let's assume that prior to working for your government employer you worked for several years in the private sector for an employer which participated in Social Security and you have accumulated the 40 quarters of work necessary to be eligible for Social Security benefits. You left that job several years ago, and now you have been working for a state or local government employer which does not pay into Social Security.

Prior to 1983, Social Security would have treated your benefits like a lower income worker who had not earned as much during the course of his or her employment, giving you a higher percentage of your preretirement earnings than someone who had a higher income. They label this extra preretirement income that you would have received under the old system as a *windfall*.

The Social Security benefits you receive are based on your average monthly earnings adjusted for inflation. Social Security divides these wages into three different amounts. For example, the first part of a 62-year-old worker's salary (one who turns 62 in 2002) would be $592, the second part would be $2,975, and the third part would be any monthly earnings in excess of that. Normally, Social Security multiplies each part by a percentage. The first part is multiplied by 90 percent, the second part is multiplied by 32 percent, and the third part is multiplied by 15 percent. If you are a state or local government employee who does not have 30 years of "substantial earnings" in a job which paid into Social Security taxes, your first $592 will be multiplied by 40 percent instead of 90 percent.

What Are Substantial Earnings?

Social Security wants to see if you have made substantial earnings from which you have paid into Social Security taxes. As you might expect, based on the cost of living and inflation, what constitutes substantial earnings has increased each year from a low of $900 a year from 1937 to 1954 to the current amount of $15,750 for 2002. You will need to determine whether the years into which you paid Social Security taxes were substantial earnings years.

If you have 30 years or more of substantial earnings paying into Social Security taxes, Social Security will use the 90 percent multiplier for the first part of your earnings. In the event that you are between 21 and 29 years of substantial earnings in a job which paid into Social Security taxes, the multiplier for the first part of your earnings will be reduced 5 percent each year from 85 percent for those with 29 years to 45 percent for those with 21 years. For those with 20 years or less of substantial earnings, the number is the flat 40 percent. For further information about what constitutes substantial earnings for a given year, take a look at Social Security Publication #05-10045, "A Pension from Work Not Covered by Social Security."

A CAPITAL IDEA. If you have worked during which time you have paid Social Security taxes but not reached the 40 quarters needed to receive Social Security benefits, you may consider working for a few quarters for another employer after you leave your government employer so that you can accumulate the additional quarters needed for obtaining Social Security benefits. Additionally, as you can see from learning about the Windfall Elimination Provision, your Social Security benefits will be reduced substantially if you worked for a government employer that did not pay into Social Security, unless you have accumulated enough years of substantial earnings while paying Social Security taxes. Therefore, if you wish to work for an employer which pays into Social Security after your government job, you should check to see if you will be making substantial earnings based on Social Security current earnings qualifications.

HOW DOES IT WORK? Social Security Offsets for Spouse's or Widow(er)'s Benefits. Social Security provides benefits to husbands or wives who have little or no Social Security benefits of their own. If your government employer does not pay into Social Security, your spouse or widow(er)'s Social Security benefits will be reduced by two-thirds of the amount paid from your government pension.

A CAPITAL IDEA. Let's assume that you get a government pension of $900 per month from an employer that did not pay into Social Security. Two-thirds of this benefit, or $600, will be used to offset your Social Security benefit of your spouse or widow(er). If your spouse was entitled to $750 per month, he or she will receive $150 per month after the offset is deducted. If a spouse is eligible for a spousal Social Security benefit and also eligible for his or her own benefit, he or she can only take the higher of the two benefits—not both. Additionally, if a spouse draws a government pension from an employer which does not pay into Social Security and is also eligible for spousal Social Security benefits from a spouse who paid into Social Security, he or she may not receive those spousal Social Security benefits.

State and Local Government Employees Who Are Exempted from the Offset

The following are exceptions to the offset:

- You worked for a government entity that was not paying into Social Security but changed over and began paying into Social Security taxes on or before your last day of employment. Some municipalities, in particular, changed over from not paying into Social Security to later paying into the program.

- Your government pension is not based on your own income.

- You were eligible to receive your government pension prior to December 1982 and you also met all of the requirements of spousal Social Security benefits that were in effect in January 1977.

APPLYING FOR SOCIAL SECURITY BENEFITS WHEN YOU RETIRE

You can apply for your Social Security benefits via the Internet, over the phone, or in person. As of the writing of this book, Social Security is currently in the process of developing applications for claims for through WEB TV and for Macintosh users. If you fit into these categories, you currently should call Social Security to apply for claims at 800-772-1213 or you can apply for benefits in person at a nearby Social Security office. You are also entitled to have someone represent you when you apply for claims.

Once you begin receiving Social Security benefits, you should let the Social Security office know if there is a change in any of the following information:

- Your name

- Your address

- Your marital status

- Your citizenship status

- Your checking account, if you receive direct deposit payments

You should also notify Social Security if one of the following events occurs:

- You leave the United States for more than 30 days

- You are no longer caring for a child who receives Social Security benefits

- You start receiving a pension from employment which was not covered by Social Security

- You find out that your estimated earnings will change

- You adopt a child

- You are no longer able to manage your funds

- You are convicted of a crime

- You pass away (Someone else should do this one.)

FOR YOUR REFERENCE. *You can contact the Social Security Administration in a variety of ways:*

Social Security Administration
Office of Earnings Operations
PO Box 33026
Baltimore, MD 21290-3026
800-772-1213
Deaf or hard of hearing: TTY 800-325-0778
<www.ssa.gov>

CHAPTER 7

YOU ARE A HIGHLY COMPENSATED GOVERNMENT EMPLOYEE OR HAVE SIMILAR NEEDS

*O*ne of the biggest misconceptions about government employees is that very few, if any, government employees make substantial earnings compared to their private sector counterparts. Nothing could be further from the truth. In fact, there are a growing number of highly compensated government employees who have specialized retirement planning needs. If you are one of these individuals, this chapter will be of special significance. Even if you are not part of this group (yet!), you will *still* want to read this section to pick up additional ideas for your government retirement plan. I have found often that employees who are not as highly compensated may have similar needs because they have been very good savers in their retirement plans

such as deferred compensation; they have spouses or life part-
ners who are highly compensated; or they come into large sums
of money from inheritance or other means.

Although it would be more convenient to use absolute figures quantifying highly compensated employees, this is very
difficult because of two issues. First, the United States Department of Labor does not break down salary statistics in that fash-
ion. Second, a salary which would be considered "highly
compensated" in one geographical region of the United States
may not be in an area with a higher cost of living.

PUBLIC WORKING KNOWLEDGE. *In 2000, the median annual income of general and operations managers for local governments was
$54,700. In that same year, the median annual income of chief executives in
local government was $69,790.*

(Source: United States Department of Labor, Bureau of Labor Statistics, Top Executives)

HOW DOES IT WORK? Appointed versus Civil Service. *Many
larger government employers will require that you take a civil service
exam for qualification for your job. These exams may consist of a written
exam, an oral exam, a performance test, or a combination of all three types
of exams. The advantage of civil service is that once you have a job and
have passed your probationary period you have very few worries about job
security.*

*Smaller government employers, as well as several larger ones, have
appointed positions that do not require you to take an exam to qualify;
however, your job security is far more questionable. In some instances,
appointed individuals will have higher compensation than their civil service
counterparts in similar jobs because their positions are more tenuous.*

SOUNDS LIKE A PLAN. *Jasmine is 42 years old and is the Solicitor General for a state legal department. She earns $150,000 a year, is appointed, has not started saving for retirement, and her husband, who is also appointed at another municipality, earns $60,000 as a city planner. Jasmine and her husband have directed most of their monies towards paying for their son's college education fund, which is presently fully funded.*

What should Jasmine consider when planning her retirement strategy?

Jasmine should consider directing her attention toward retirement planning now that she has completed her educational planning for her son. Because Jasmine is an appointed official, her job is not as secure as a civil service employee. She should harness her high salary now and immediately establish a 457 plan with her state. Jasmine should contribute the maximum $11,000 a year into her 457 plan. She and her husband may also wish to consider establishing an annuity, which will create an additional tax deferred account with which to grow her retirement assets.

PUBLIC WORKING KNOWLEDGE.*The concept of using civil service examinations for government positions dates back to ancient civilizations. In fact, the fascinating book,* China's Examination Hell: The Civil Service Examinations of Imperial China *by Ichisada Miyazaki (New York: Weatherhill, 1976) recounts the grueling tasks facing potential civil servants through the course of several dynasties. For example, The Palace Examination, which originated during the T'ang dynasty, was characterized by exceedingly long questions which were written in a very solemn style. If you thought your civil service exams were challenging, you were not alone.*

SHOULD YOU BE WORKING WITH A PROFESSIONAL OR ON YOUR OWN?

If you are a highly compensated government employee or you have come into a large amount of money through inheritance or other means, you may be wondering whether you should be managing your money or turning that over to a professional. The good news is that there are a wide variety of options available to you. Let's look at each of these options.

Option 1: Going It on Your Own

If you picked up this book, there is a strong chance that you are someone who likes to be well informed and do your homework. This is a good thing! You may have had experience with financial professionals in the past or you may have even worked in the brokerage industry prior to your government employment. If you believe that you have the proper amount of experience to handle the coordination of your financial needs, you should do it on your own. Hopefully, this book has given you some extra insights into your government retirement. Additionally, you may wish to use a discount brokerage house for your stock trades. The commissions for these trades will be a fraction of what full-service brokerage houses charge, but you generally will not receive any advice regarding the trade.

Option 2: Investing in Mutual Funds (Either Load or No-Load) by Yourself

You do not require a financial advisor or broker to purchase mutual funds for yourself or your family, either in your retirement accounts or nonretirement (often known as "retail") accounts. As discussed earlier, mutual funds are professionally run and will manage your money through a variety of ways including investing in groups of stocks, bonds, or a combination of the two.

There are a vast number of both load (commission paid) and no-load funds from which you may choose. If you construct your own portfolio by buying mutual funds, you may select either actively managed funds or passively managed funds such as index funds. Remember, no matter what funds you select either load or no-load, you will still pay operational expenses to the fund in addition to any commissions you are charged to get into the fund (if it is a load fund).

Option 3: Join an Investment Club

An investment club can be a beautiful thing if all of the individuals in the club are motivated and each member does his or her job to prepare for group meetings and relays the research he or she conducted to the other club members promptly. Investment clubs also carry the added benefits of exposing you to different ideas and strategies you wouldn't have come up with in a vacuum on your own. If you decide to invest your money in a "pooled account" (something I generally would recommend against), make certain that you *really* trust the individual or individuals who are running the club. After all, it is your money and you want to make sure that it stays that way!

Option 4: Hire a Financial Advisor

As a financial advisor at a full-service brokerage house, I certainly have a bias here and I obviously believe that this option is appropriate for many investors. But it may not be right for everybody. A financial advisor is an individual whose goals should be to create a plan of action for your finances, implement that plan once you have agreed to it, and continually update the plan as your personal needs and market conditions change. The backgrounds of financial advisors vary widely including credentials such as Certified Financial Planners (CFPs) and attorneys. In fact, many financial advisors come from myriad professions and bring that experience to the table.

Individuals with higher net worth will often gravitate towards financial advisors simply because there is far more at stake if an investment miscalculation is made that will affect large sums of money. Ideally, the financial advisor should provide a highly informed outlook on your finances and should be emotionally detached when selecting and, at times, getting rid of certain types of investments.

Selection Criteria

- *Do you feel comfortable with this individual?* This is a tough one, yet it is probably one of the most critical questions you can ask when choosing a financial advisor. Sometimes you get a feeling in the pit of your stomach that for whatever reason this is or is not going to be a good working relationship. Trust your gut instinct.

- *How much experience does this person have?* Again, it is difficult to judge how much experience someone has simply by the number of years they have worked as a financial advisor. That being said, you don't need to be anyone's guinea pig if you can avoid it. Look for financial advisors with a minimum of three years experience professionally advising individuals about finances. If you have any questions as to how long the person has been advising professionally, ask him or her the date they became licensed and what licensing he or she possesses.

- *How much are this person's fees and how are they motivated to do business?* The brokerage industry has changed radically over the past ten years. Although there are still many financial advisors or brokers who are "transactionalists," meaning they earn their living by trading in and out of stocks, the trend has been away from that and towards "managed money." Unlike transactionalists, financial advisors who invest their clients' money using managed money programs or "wrap" business derive their commission or "gross" from a percentage of the overall assets under management (that's the wrap) which you negotiate with the advisor. The advantage of this commission structure is that there is no financial incentive for the financial advisor to advocate moving funds when it may not be advisable. This person's goals are also aligned with yours in that he or she wants your money to grow just as much as you do because his or her commission goes up as the account size increases.

SOUNDS LIKE A PLAN. *Justin is a married 39-year-old hospital administrator at a public hospital, making $120,000 year. He recently started his current job, having left a biotech company that had a 401(k) to which he contributed till it grew to $200,000. He and his stay-at-home wife have three small children and have accumulated $500,000 in savings. Justin feels that he has a good handle on his finances, but he would like a second opinion and direction for his retirement planning.*

What should Justin consider when planning his retirement strategy?

Justin's biggest quandary is one that faces a large number of high-net-worth and high-income earners: Do I really need to spend the money to do something I have been doing myself: managing my money? The answer to this question depends on how complex Justin's financial goals are, including retirement planning, educational planning for his children, insurance planning (particularly since Justin is the sole wage earner and his wife and children are all dependent on his earning potential), and ultimately his estate planning. Justin may consider meeting with a financial planner and/or an investment advisor to see whether his strategy is on track. If his job carries long hours, he may not have adequate time to devote to making sure all of his financial planning is both created and executed on a regular and systematic basis. If this is the case, he should select someone whose credentials, accessibility, and ability to teach new financial information align with both his and his spouse's financial goals.

Areas that Justin may also wish to consider are whether to roll over his 401(k) into an IRA or into his current employer's 403(b) plan. He should determine which option is not only most cost effective with the fewest fees, but also should balance this with the quality and diversity of offerings he has in his plans. For example, Justin's current 403(b) can only be invested in mutual funds, whereas his former 401(k) (if it contained a self-directed brokerage account) or IRA rollover may be invested using individual stocks, bonds, and/or mutual funds.

MANAGED MONEY PROGRAMS

Managed money programs, particularly for individuals with several hundred thousand dollars or more to invest, provide a way to access institutional-level money managers under the guidance of a financial advisor. You can place your IRA investments into managed money as well as into funds in your nonretirement or retail accounts. If done correctly, managed money will provide you with potential advantages over mutual funds including outright stock ownership and the ability to custom tailor your portfolio to avoid certain investments such as tobacco companies. Ideally, the financial advisor will let you know if there is a problem with one of the money managers, just as she would regarding a mutual fund, and then recommend moving to another investment option.

UNCLE SAM'S CUT. *If you decide to use managed money for your nonretirement accounts, you can often custom design your investment platform so that it is more tax-efficient or "tax managed." What this means is that your portfolio will be more concerned with achieving its investment objectives by doing fewer stock trades therefore causing* *fewer capital gains on which you will have to pay taxes. If you use managed money in retirement accounts such as IRA rollovers, tax efficiency will not be a major concern because your account is housed in a tax-deferred shell.*

Other Considerations: College Funding

Paying for your children's college education is certainly not a concern limited to the highly compensated government employee. In fact, millions of parents are in the process of trying to save for their children's college education. So, what ways exist to save for college education?

UTMA/UGMA Accounts

Depending on the state in which you reside, you may save for your child's college education by setting up a custodial account. This account has the advantages of no contribution limits and tremendous flexibility of investment options.

And the downside is? One of the major disadvantages of the custodial account is that the money inside is taxable each year, so if you have mutual funds which are giving off capital gains you will be taxed on these gains each year. Another major disadvantage from the vantage point of the parent is that when the minor reaches the age of majority he or she has total control over how to spend the money inside the account—not you the faithful parent(s) who have been making sacrifices to create a pot of money for educational purposes.

The Coverdell Educational Savings Account

The Coverdell Educational Savings Account allows you to contribute $2,000 per year for educational purposes into an account that grows without any taxes. The new tax laws allow this money to be withdrawn tax-free if used for educational purposes. It should also be noted that the tax laws that permit this tax-free withdrawal are part of a sunset provision that lasts until 2010. It is considered unlikely by industry experts that Congress will change these rules, so many parents have come to rely on this savings vehicle for funding their children's college education.

The major drawback of the Coverdell Educational Savings Account is that it allows you to save only $2,000 a year. One advantage is that, unlike the 529 Plan (which we discuss next), it can be used for educational expenses arising prior to college such as private preschool expenses. This feature together with a wide variety of investment options which grow tax exempt make this a nice alternative for college savings. The new tax laws permit you to have both a Coverdell and a 529 Plan without incurring penalties, which was not previously allowed.

The 529 Plan

Congress recognized that the Coverdell was severely limited with its small annual maximum contribution limit (in fact, until 2002, the maximum educational IRA contribution was a whopping $500 a year). For that reason, they allowed every state in the country to create their own 529 Plan for college education savings. There are currently 42 states that offer 529 Plans and more 529 Plans are currently being created.

HOW DOES IT WORK? 529 Plans. *529 Plans work similar to Coverdell Educational Savings Accounts in that you are contributing money towards your child or nephew's or grandchild's post–high school education. However, under the 529 you can contribute (depending on the state) a total of as much as $269,000. Check with your state to see how high your maximum annual contributions and total contributions can be. Although your total contributions cannot exceed the maximum for the state you select, your money can grow and obviously exceed that total contribution. The money placed inside the 529 is able to grow without taxes and based on the new tax law changes, you can now withdraw this money tax-free if you use it for an approved educational institution. These institutions include two-year and four-year colleges as well as graduate schools.*

THE BOTTOM LINE. *If you set up a 529 for a child or other beneficiary (such as a grandchild or nephew) you will be the owner. This means that even after the child reaches the age of majority you will have total control over the use of these funds. Additionally, you can change beneficiaries of the 529 in the event that the child decides not to attend college or does not wish to use the funds in ways that you desire.*

PUBLIC WORKING KNOWLEDGE. *The 529 market is growing in leaps and bounds. It is currently estimated by Cerulli Associates that contributions into 529 Plans will exceed $50 billion over the next five years.*

(Source: The Ultimate 529 Guide *by Barbara Kiviat, Mutual Funds, June 2002, p. 52.)*

What to Consider When Shopping for 529 Plans

Your first consideration is whether your state grants a state income tax deduction if you use its state plan. If you are granted that state deduction you should look at your own state's plan first before exploring other state's 529 plans.

If your state does not grant a tax break for choosing its plan, you should then begin comparing 529 Plans the way you shopped around for your government deferred compensation provider. Consider such criteria as the fees charged by the plan to participants, the flexibility of the plan, and whether you will have someone easily accessible who can assist you in the event that you have questions.

One thing to keep in mind when examining 529 Plans is that they are often invested in one or more sets of mutual fund families. The flexibility of investments in these plans has broadened more recently. Many 529 Plans have age-based portfolios which shift in asset allocation from more aggressive investments such as equity-based mutual funds to more conservative investments such as bonds as the child reaches the age when he or she will need to tap into the money for college.

The Use of 529 Plans as Estate Planning Tools

If you are not a highly compensated government employee but have parents who are or who were highly compensated, you may wish to let them know they can reduce their taxable estate by funding your child's 529 Plan.

UNCLE SAM'S CUT. *Under the tax laws, you are allowed to gift up to $11,000 a year without having to pay taxes. Using a 529 Plan, you can accelerate gifting for up to five years. This money will be taken out of your taxable estate, but if you die before the five-year period is up, you have to put back whatever money you gifted that was prorated into the estate. For example, if you gift $55,000 and you pass away in year 3, $22,000, or the money from the last two years you did not live, will return into your taxable estate.*

Additionally, once you accelerate gifting, you cannot gift for the number of years in which you have accelerated. If you accelerated for five years, you must wait five years until you gift again.

Long-Term Care

Well, now that you've saved for your kids' college educations what about saving for your senior years? Long-term care allows you make sure that you are taken care of if you need in-home or nursing care in your senior years.

LIFE OR POLICY. *Long-term care is an insurance product that comes with a number of different bells and whistles including death benefits in the event that you pass away. Some newer long-term care products are moving away from the "use it or lose it" idea and actually provide a cash value for their policies.*

THE BOTTOM LINE. *Like disability insurance, long-term care is expensive. You may want to see if your government employer has any special rates based on the economy of scale. It is critical that you do your* homework with this policy, and if you choose to work with a financial advisor on long-term care make certain that he or she explains everything you do not understand in detail.

My Fifth ME Page

Me: The Highly Compensated Government Employee or Similarly Situated

1. My name is _____.

2. Today's date is _____.

3. My current age is _____.

4. My current government employer is _____.

5. My annual income is $_____.

6. Using a 1 (lowest) to 10 (highest) scale, my investing experience is a _____.

7. I have alternative sources of income. ( ) Yes ( ) No

(continued)

My Fifth ME Page *(continued)*

8. If yes, I have the following:

   a. Rental property $_____ (total/year)

   b. Side business activities $_____ (total/year)

   c. Other _____ $_____ (total/year)

9. My spouse or life partner works. ( ) Yes ( ) No

10. If yes, he/she makes $ _____ per year.

11. I am vested in my pension. ( ) Yes ( ) No

12. I have funded a 529 Plan because I have children or others
    for whom I wish to pay the costs of higher education.
    ( ) Yes ( ) No

13. I have an estate plan in place. ( ) Yes ( ) No

14. I have examined long-term care insurance. ( ) Yes ( ) No

15. I have a living trust or a will. ( ) Yes ( ) No

CHAPTER 8

YOU ARE A MEMBER OF THE POLICE FORCE OR FIRE DEPARTMENT

Working with sworn police officers and firefighters can present an interesting set of challenges for newer retirement plan representatives under the naive impression that safety jobs are parallel to the nonsafety jobs in a municipality. At the most basic level, the shift hours for sworn police officers and firefighters are vastly different simply because these two departments must be staffed 24 hours a day, 7 days a week.

As an individual trying to convey investment advice, it can also be interesting when you're in the middle of a speech and suddenly an alarm goes off calling every firefighter in the room to an emergency. Personally, what working with safety personnel has taught me is that these brave men and women who devote and often risk their lives to save others are an exceptionally special group of people. And if you are among this group, you have special government retirement needs.

PUBLIC WORKING KNOWLEDGE. *Innovative Silicon Valley city Sunnyvale, California, cross-trains both firefighters and police officers to be able to perform each other's jobs. Not surprisingly, the individuals performing these jobs are among the most highly paid safety workers in the country.*

SAFETY TIME HORIZONS

Retirement benefits for firefighters and police are generally not comparable to nonsafety employees simply because their expected time spent on the job and in their profession is generally shorter than their nonsafety counterparts. In fact, in California, a movement has been underway for the CalPers (State of California Pension Plan) system to allow police officers to retire at 50 years of age with 3 percent of their salary for every year served. With a goal of retiring at such a young age, how do you calibrate your retirement savings strategy?

Retirement Strategies and Risk Tolerances

As a nonsafety private sector employee, I never would have understood how much members of the safety field come to depend on each other on a daily basis until I was actually physically present watching them in action. Firefighters and police must trust their coworkers because more than a good job is on the line. Lives are on the line—the lives of potential victims and their own lives. So I realize that safety workers seek out information from each other and trust that advice.

However, I have to caution you that it is critical not to choose investment options because a coworker advises such, simply because you may not have the same risk tolerance, time horizon, or other investment needs. But because teamwork is such an integral part of your job, I have included two ways of working on retirement that should work well for you, in addition to doing it all on your own or with a financial advisor.

Investment Teamwork for Safety Workers

In watching how members of both the police and fire departments often compare notes regarding investments such as mutual funds, I recommend the following two strategies if you wish to work as a team.

The Buddy System Investor

Try to find an investment partner who is closest to you in age, risk tolerance, and anticipated time of service. It would be ideal if this individual also has similar investment experience. The key to making sure your portfolio is running smoothly is to keep it manageable. If you decide to form an investment buddy team, each of you should limit the number of investments so that you have enough investment categories covered—such as small capitalization value, large capitalization growth, and bond funds— but not so many that you can't track them all.

From my experience, the average investor generally uses between four and seven mutual funds to properly diversify his or her portfolio. If you choose six funds, each buddy should make it his or her business to track three funds. That way you will work as an investment team.

The Total Team Investment Strategy

Let's assume that your entire firehouse wants to function as an investment team, similar to an investment club but centered around tracking your retirement portfolios. The first obstacle you will encounter is individual risk tolerance and the potential for misguiding members of the team who gravitate toward the higher performing, sometimes very aggressive funds, selected by your other team members. In an effort to avoid this, be sure to group your investment options into categories including low, medium, and high risk tolerance. If you are unsure what the risk tolerances are for particular funds, do not hesitate to contact your rep or the fund companies directly.

SAFETY DEFINED BENEFIT PENSIONS

Safety personnel are often given different vesting and percentage amounts of their overall salaries than their nonsafety counterparts. For example, several municipalities offer sworn police officers 3 percent for every year worked by 50 years old.

The Retirement Strategy for Overtime Pay

The way that many firefighters and police officers often increase their salaries substantially is through putting in for overtime work when it's available. This money can certainly come in handy when there are extra bills at home. In fact, this money can also come in hand when you are planning your safety retirement strategy.

THE BOTTOM LINE. *You never want to feel strapped by how much you put into your retirement account. You are not saving for retirement to impress your accountant or your stockbroker or even yourself. You are saving for retirement to achieve a goal of financial security in the years when you are no longer working. Keeping this in mind, if you are making overtime money, you are best served (after your regular day to day expenses and extra expenses such as vacation trips) by putting some of this money aside for retirement or other needs. You may consider establishing an IRA in addition to your 457 plan. If you are contributing money into your IRA and it is nondeductible, you should file IRS form 8606 with your tax return.*

SOUNDS LIKE A PLAN. *Fred is a 40-year-old firefighter who started with his municipality as a full-time employee when he was 27. He has four children and a wife. He puts in a great deal of overtime, but he wants to retire as soon as he turns 50.*

What should Fred consider when planning his retirement strategy?

Like the vast majority of state and local government workers, Fred's primary retirement asset is his defined benefit pension plan, which will act to replace a substantial percentage of his current salary. For example, if Fred currently earns $65,000 a year and his defined benefit pension plan *provides 3 percent a year for safety employees, he will have 23 years when he retires, or 23 x 3 = 69 percent of his income. He will need to replace the 31 percent that he will lose. However, this amount may be less, depending on the tax treatment of his pension in his state of residence. Fred should view this pension as a generator that will create new monies each month, which he will need to supplement from income using other sources. Because Fred will be retiring at 50, he will not be eligible for Social Security at the time he leaves service. Fred should consider using his additional overtime income as an income generator for when he goes into retirement.*

INSURANCE OR DEFERRED COMPENSATION: WHICH COMES FIRST?

When the stock markets look scarier than facing a burning building or a hostage situation, it is tempting to try to cut bait and move the money out. So a new strategy of pulling money out of deferred compensation contributions and putting it toward insurance premiums has cropped up. Is this the best strategy? Generally not. Your deferred compensation plan is a benefit for you in that it defers money from your taxable income and also (hopefully) grows the money tax-deferred.

I am not saying that you should not plan for insurance considerations, which are discussed next. However, in order of priority you should fund your deferred compensation before using your deferred compensation contributions to fund insurance premiums. After you have funded your deferred compensation plan, you should turn your attention to your insurance needs.

Insurance Considerations

LIFE OR POLICY? *Although there is no question that every government worker's job is an important one no matter in what part of the municipality he or she works, there are different degrees of risk associated with different positions. For example, a librarian may encounter an irate library patron who is unable to find a particular book. Generally, this will not result in a physical attack. Both firefighters and sworn officers are put in potentially dangerous situations on a regular basis. Therefore, they need to protect themselves and their loved ones with some forms of insurance.*

Disability Insurance

In the event that you get injured, you may qualify for worker's compensation. Additionally, you may be eligible for Social Security insurance; however, the criteria for receiving Social Security disability benefits are rather stringent.

HOW DOES IT WORK? *Disability insurance protects you in the event that you lose one of your greatest assets—your ability to earn a living. In the event that you are disabled, the insurance will create an income stream for you. But before you run out and buy this rather expensive form of insurance, there are a few things to look at first.*

There are a number of considerations you must take into account when purchasing disability insurance. One of the most important considerations is the length of the elimination period, which is the period of time until your disability benefits begin. The amount of money you will want to keep as a cash reserve is tied into the length of this elimination period. An additional consideration is whether you are insured for the loss of being able to do your own occupation or the lower-experience alternative of being insured for any occupation which your skill set will allow you to perform.

 SOUNDS LIKE A PLAN. *Jenny is 25 years old and married to a man studying to be a social worker. She just joined the police force as a sworn officer for a small municipality. She had been working at a larger city as a reference librarian prior to her new job as a sworn officer, but she wanted a change of location and careers.*

What should Jenny consider when creating her retirement strategy?

Like many government employees who transfer from small to large municipalities, the main concern when deciding how to coordinate assets is evaluating your former plan(s) versus your new plan(s). Many larger municipalities have multiple providers, which means more choices and the need to do your homework when looking at the types of funds offered, the fees charged, and the ability to move assets. Jenny should find out if she can pick and choose among the plans and take the best features from each plan. If she likes the idea of consolidating into one plan, she should make certain that the investments offered are solid in all categories, such as a strong, large capitalization growth fund and a good international value fund. Larger municipality plans may have lower fees than their smaller municipal counterparts based on economy of scale.

An additional consideration for Jenny is her need for insurance planning, because currently she is the sole support for her family, and she has shifted from a lower risk job as a librarian to a sworn officer. Jenny should explore both life and disability insurance options offered through her municipality and professional peace officer organizations.

PUBLIC WORKING KNOWLEDGE. *Cardiac arrest is among the leading causes of firefighter disability in the United States today.*

FOR YOUR REFERENCE. Web sites for firefighters. *Below are four strong Web sites for firefighters that provide up-to-date information on a variety of issues that firefighters will find useful.*

- FireHouse.com *<www.firehouse.com> An outstanding resource about things firefighters want to learn most ranging from current news stories to special information for EMTs.*

- International Association of Firefighters (AFL-CIO) *<www.iaff.org> This well-organized site provides members with information about legislation, union benefits, and other issues of interest to the firefighting community.*

- Women Firefighter's Resource Page *<www.wfsi.org> This informative site is specifically designed for women firefighters.*

- FireDepartment.Net *<www.firedept.net> FireDepartment.Net is an Internet service provider which has links to a number of important Web sites such as the National Fire Weather Center, employment opportunities, and training sites.*

Web sites for police officers. *While it is impossible to list all of the great Web sites specially designed for law enforcement officers across the entire United States, the following are outstanding Web sites and should be rather helpful to you.*

- Fraternal Order of Police *<www.grandlodgefop.org> This national organization founded in 1915, is open to all full-time sworn officers with arrest power employed by a government entity and currently has 299,000 members.*

- NYSCOPBA. *(New York State Correctional Officers and Police Benevolent Society) <www.nyscopba.org> This organization provides a number of benefits to its members including offering information* *specific to New York state retirement benefits as well as life and disability insurance options.*

- Policepay.Net *<www.policepay.net> This Web site publishes data on a monthly wage survey index of the 150 largest police departments in the United States.*

- PORAC *(Peace Officers Research Association of California) <www.porac.org> PORAC is one of the largest associations of peace officers on the West Coast and in the United States. This Web site is exceptionally helpful in terms of providing training and legislative information helpful to peace officers as well as employment listings. This organization also offers group insurance benefits for its members.*

- TMPA *(Texas Municipal Police Association) <www.tmpa.org> Texas Municipal Police Association provides a number of services both in education and through insurance benefits for its member peace officers.*

My Sixth ME Page

Me, A Safety Employee

1. My name is _____.

2. Today's date is _____.

3. I am ___ years old; I make $ _____ year; I currently defer
   $_____ per year into my deferred compensation plan.

4. I have $ _____ as my deferred compensation balance
   at my current municipality.

5. I have $ _____ in total (if you have separate balances
   list them and add them up) balances for my deferred compensation plans at other municipalities or 403(b)s and 401(k)s.

6. The municipality where I currently work is _____.

7. I have an investment buddy. ( ) Yes ( ) No

8. If yes, his/her name is _____.

9. I am on an investment team. ( ) Yes ( ) No

(continued)

My Sixth ME Page *(continued)*

10. If yes, my team members are

_____

_____

_____

11. There are individuals who rely on me for financial support, such as a spouse and/or children. ( ) Yes ( ) No

12. I have planned for my insurance needs (including disability and life insurance). ( ) Yes ( ) No

13. My municipality or fire/police association provides group insurance. ( ) Yes ( ) No

The amount of my group insurance policy is $_____.

CHAPTER 9

THE ME PAGES

Putting It All Together

*T*his final section is all about you. As you are now aware from reading up to this point, there is a great deal to learn as a state or local government employee about your retirement investing and planning. Many of the areas I have covered are applicable to every state and local government employee in the United States. However, the take-home message I want you to get from this book is that you are an individual with individual needs. That's where the Me Pages come in. You have been filling out Me Pages in other sections of this book. But you may have said to yourself, "How does this all fit together?" Well, now you're going to find out. Assembling the information from your Me Pages in the sections provided in this chapter will make it far easier for you to actually plan your retirement, no matter how many years you have until you anticipate retiring. Remember this word: *anticipate.* You may plan on retiring in 20 years, but find that for whatever reason you decide to retire in 22 years. Or if you plan very carefully and invest wisely, you can shave that 20 years down to 18. Just imagine—two extra years without having to work. Makes you want to launch right into those Me Pages right now, doesn't it?

So, get out your pen and some scratch paper and let's begin putting your Me Pages together.

You will want to revisit these pages periodically to see if your conditions and/or goals have changed. For example, if you

I. What Will I Need to Retire?

In this section, you are putting together the basic information regarding the annual costs of your current lifestyle.

1. I anticipate retiring in _____ years.

2. My current annual living expenses are as follows:

    a. Rent/mortgage $_____/month × 12 = $_____.

    b. Taxes (including property taxes) $_____/month × 12 = $_____.

    c. Utilities $_____/month × 12 = $_____.

    d. Debt servicing (including student loans, outstanding credit cards, and/or other debt obligations) = $_____/ month × 12 = $_____.

e. Computers, books, and periodicals $ _____/ year.

f. Food $_____/month × 12 = $_____.

g. Educational care $_____/ year.

h. Transportation costs $_____/month × 12 = $_____.

i. Clothing $_____/year.

j. Insurance costs (including automobile/homeowners/renters/life/disability) $_____/month × 12 = $ _____.

k. Miscellaneous luxury expenses (including movies, cable TV, vacations, and restaurants) = $ _____/month × 12 = $ _____.

l. Charitable expenses = $_____/year.

m. Pet expenses $ _____/year.

n. Medical and Dental expenses $ _____/year.

o. Gifts (birthday, holiday, etc.) $_____/year.

p. Alimony/child support $_____/year.

q. Total (add up all those that apply to you) $_____/year.

r. Total after retirement $_____/year.

are currently single and later get married you may want to amend your annual income to take into account your spouse's income.

You now have an approximation of your current annual living expenses. If you choose to move to a less expensive region in the country you may cut back on these expenses. Additionally, expenses that you have now may not exist by the time you retire such as mortgage payments. Now, circle those items that you will assume will no longer exist when you are at retirement age. Subtract those amounts from your total (Line q) and put that number on the Total after retirement line (Line r).

PUBLIC WORKING KNOWLEDGE. *Although you may assume that your expenses will dramatically decrease when you retire, it is a sobering fact that a recent study by Georgia State University indicates that household spending only decreases slightly upon reaching the retirement years. In fact, the study found that among those with $40,000 annual incomes expenses dropped only $484 per year for those individuals who went into retirement; and households with $90,000 annual incomes decreased their expenses in retirement by only $1,022 per year.*

II. The Ways I Will Fund My Retirement

A. My Government (Defined Benefit) Pension: The Bedrock of My Retirement

1. I am eligible for a government defined benefit pension?
   ( ) Yes ( ) No

2. I have currently been with my government employer _____ years.

3. My current government pension vests in _____ years.

4. I anticipate working at my current job _____ years.

5. Assuming a 5 percent increase in salary for each year, my current salary for my final year of employment (or the average of my last number of years if my government employer calculates in that manner) will be $_____.

6. The percentage of my income I will be entitled to as pension based on the election I selected (based on my current situation) is _____ percent.

7. Multiply line 5 by line 6 = $_____ per year.

B. My Other Defined Benefit Pensions (If Applicable)

Sometimes, you may be able to consolidate pension plans particularly from municipalities in the same state. However, if this is not an option or if you have nongovernment pensions, you will have to track them separately.

Pension 2

1. I have worked at this job _____ years.

2. My pension is vested. ( ) Yes ( ) No

(continued)

II. Ways I Will Fund My Retirement (continued)

3. If yes, my final income or the average of that income if that is what this job uses to determine my pension was

    $_____.

4. The percentage of my income to which I am entitled is _____ percent.

5. Multiply line 3 by line 4 = $_____ per year.

Pension 3

1. I have worked at this job _____ years.

2. My pension is vested. ( ) Yes ( ) No

3. If yes, my final income or the average of that income if that is what this job uses to determine my pension was

    $_____.

4. The percentage of my income to which I am entitled is _____ percent.

5. Multiply line 3 by line 4 = $_____ per year.

III. Deferred Compensation

My Defined Contribution Plan(s)

A. My Current Government Deferred Compensation 457/403(b) Plan

1. The current balance in my 457/403(b) plan is $_____.

2. I am currently contributing per year $_____ to my 457/403(b) plan.

3. I anticipate contributing to my 457/403(b) plan for _____ more years.

4. If you are invested in the stock and/or bond markets the performance of your investments will vary but as a general rule of thumb calculate your contributions from Line 2 and multiply by the number of years you will be contributing from Line 3 = $_____.

   a. For conservative investors: Multiply the number you arrived at on Line 6 by 1.05 as a conservative estimate (without compounding) of your money $_____.
   (Obviously this is an approximation; depending on market performance and compounding the number may be higher or lower.)

(continued)

III. Deferred Compensation *(continued)*

b. For moderate investors: Multiply the number you arrive at on Line 6 by 1.08 as a moderate estimate (without compounding) of your money $_____.
(Obviously this is an approximation; depending on market performance and compounding the number may be higher or lower.)

c. For aggressive investors: Multiply the number you arrive at on Line 6 by 1.12 as an aggressive estimate (without compounding) of your money $_____.
(Obviously this is an approximation; depending on market performance and compounding the number may be higher or lower.)

B. My Other Government/Nongovernment Entity Deferred Compensation (457, 401(k), and 403(b)) Plans

You may wish to consolidate these plans or your 401(k) plan if your current government employer has a 457/403(b) which is comparable or better to the one(s) in which you have participated. However, if you don't consolidate use the following:

Deferred Compensation Plan 2

1. The government/nongovernment entity is _____.

2. My current balance is $_____.

3. I will have $_____ in this account when I retire in _____ years. (Assuming same as above and you do not take distributions from this account.)

Deferred Compensation Plan 3

1. The government/nongovernment entity is _____.

2. My current balance is $_____.

3. I will have $_____ in this account when I retire in _____ years. (Assuming same as above and you do not take distributions from this account.)

Deferred Compensation Plan 4

1. The government/nongovernment entity is _____.

2. My current balance is $_____.

3. I will have $_____ in this account when I retire in _____ years. (Assuming same as above and you do not take distributions from this account.)

(continued)

III. Deferred Compensation *(continued)*

C. My Individual Retirement Accounts (Including but Not Limited to SEP, SIMPLE, Traditional, and Roth IRAs)

IRA 1

1. The account is held in _____.

2. It is a _____ IRA.

3. This money came from a rollover from a 457, 403(b), or 401(k).
   ( ) Yes ( ) No

4. If yes, which type of plan rolled into this IRA? _____

5. The current balance of this account is $_____.

IRA 2

1. The account is held in _____.

2. It is a _____ IRA.

3. This money came from a rollover from a 457, 403(b), or 401(k).
   ( ) Yes ( ) No

4. If yes, which type of plan rolled into this IRA? _____

5. The current balance of this account is $_____.

D. Social Security

1. I have worked 40 quarters for an entity where I have paid into Social Security. ( ) Yes ( ) No

2. I am currently entitled to $_____/year at the time I anticipate retiring in _____ years.

3. I have worked for a government employer which is not paying into Social Security. ( ) Yes ( ) No

4. If yes, check to see if your Social Security benefits are reduced and by how much.

5. I am eligible for spousal Social Security benefits. ( ) Yes ( ) No

6. If yes, check to see if your Social Security benefits are reduced and by how much.

E. Social Security Substitutes

Several government employers that do not pay into Social Security have plans that help their employees put money aside in lieu of Social Security.

1. The current balance in my substitute plan is $_____.

2. How much is currently being contributed $_____ per year to my plan.

(continued)

III. Deferred Compensation (continued)

3. I anticipate being in my plan _____ more years.

4. If you are invested in the stock and/or bond markets the performance of your investments will vary, but as a general rule of thumb calculate your contributions from Line 2 and multiply by the number of years you will be contributing from Line 3 = $_____.

   a. For conservative investors: Multiply the number you arrive at on Line 4 by 1.05 as a conservative estimate (without compounding) of your money $_____. (Obviously this is an approximation; depending on market performance and compounding the number may be higher or lower.)

   b. For moderate investors: Multiply the number you arrive at on Line 4 by 1.08 as a moderate estimate (without com-pounding) of your money $_____. (Obviously this is an approximation; depending on market performance and compounding the number may be higher or lower.)

   c. For aggressive investors: Multiply the number you arrive at on Line 4 by 1.12 as an aggressive estimate (without com-pounding) of your money $_____. (Obviously this is an approximation; depending on market performance and compounding the number may be higher or lower.)

5. I have outstanding loans against the balance of this plan.

   ( ) Yes ( ) No

6. If yes, my outstanding loan balance is $ _____ .

IV. Potential Retirement Income from All Sources

1. My defined benefit pension income (from all pensions) will be

   $ _____/year.

2. My distributions from 457, 403(b), 401(k), and 401(a) plan(s)

   (including all distributions) will be $ _____/year.

3. My distributions from IRAs (including SEP, SIMPLE, traditional,

   and Roth IRAs) will be $ _____/year.

4. My Social Security benefits will be $_____/year.

5. My other sources of income (including rental property and

   investments) will be $ _____/year.

6. My total retirement income will be (add Lines 1 through 5)

   $_____/year.

Now compare Line 2r from Section I to Line 6 in Section IV. This will show you whether you meet your retirement income needs, or experience a shortfall or a surplus.

INDEX

Bulk Pricing Information

For special discounts on
20 or more copies of this book,
call Dearborn Trade Special Sales
at 800-621-9621, extension 4455
or e-mail bermel@dearborn.com.
You'll receive great service
and top discounts.

For added visibility, please
consider our custom cover service,
which highlights your firm's name
and logo on the cover.
We are also an excellent resource
for dynamic and
knowledgeable speakers.

Dearborn™
Trade Publishing
A **Kaplan Professional** Company